AF560665

TOURISM PROMOTION

By

Thomas Walsh

DISCOVERY PUBLISHING HOUSE PVT. LTD.
NEW DELHI-110 002

Published by:
Tilak Wasan

DISCOVERY PUBLISHING HOUSE PVT. LTD.
4831/24, Ansari Road, Prahlad Street
Darya Ganj, New Delhi-110002 (India)
Phone: +91-11-23279245, 43764432
Fax: +91-11-23253475
E-mail: parul.wasan@gmail.com
discoverypublishinghouse@gmail.com
info@discoverypublishinggroup.com
web: www.discoverypublishinggroup.com

***First Edition:* 2011**
Reprinted: 2017

ISBN: 978-81-8356-890-6

Tourism Promotion

Printed in:
INDIA

PREFACE

The Indian Ministry of Tourism launched the Incredible India campaign in 2002 to encourage visitors from around the world to experience India. The concerted marketing effort included print, radio and television ads. The campaign also included road shows, which were planned for the UK, Canada, Singapore, Malaysia, Russia, Australia and New Zealand. The successful campaign received attention and praise from travel professionals and is credited with increasing the number of tourists to the nation within just a few years.

Tourism is one of the largest & important industry which is useful for the development of a nation. It occupies 11% of the world's GDP and may create 7 million new jobs by the year 2010. $595 billions have been generated by the international tourism industry in 2000. Tourism in India has grown very much during the last decades. It gives the second highest net foreign exchange earnings to our economy. Foreign tourist arrivals are at 2.64 millions during 2000. Domestic tourism helps to understand various cultures and to experience national integration among the citizens.

India has been a destination for travelers for millennia, but poor infrastructure and the lack of certain amenities have kept the tourist economy from developing further. The global marketing campaign brought India to the attention of millions of potential tourists worldwide, as the Ministry of Tourism placed print, radio and television ads in markets around the world.

CONTENTS

1

INTRODUCTION

Promotion is about telling people what's on offer. It is not entirely separate from the product because what is said and how it is said influences how the product is seen. It's 'the sizzle not the sausages' that is sold, or it's Coke with all the images of sun, youth, vitality, and world-wide harmony. It's certainly not 'carbonated water with vegetable extracts'. Promotion includes advertising (dealt with under its own heading below) but also includes direct mail, public relations, printed brochures, presence at travel trade shows, and participation in joint marketing schemes. Promotion can be very expensive and it is often difficult to decide whether or not it is successful.

Promotion of Tourism in India

In the past decade, tourism has become one of India's fastest growing markets, contributing to millions of service industry jobs. The Ministry of Tourism launched the Incredible India campaign in 2002, promoting India as a premier vacation spot. The campaign was successful, and now India is one of the top destinations for travelers from the U.S. and Canada. In August 2009 outbreaks of swine flu threatened India's late summer tourist season. Many travelers canceled trips rather than risk infection. Still, fears have now subsided and tourism seems to be growing steadily.

Incredible India Campaign

The Indian Ministry of Tourism launched the Incredible India campaign in 2002 to encourage visitors from around the world to experience India. The concerted marketing effort included print, radio and television ads. The campaign also included road shows, which were planned for the UK, Canada, Singapore, Malaysia, Russia, Australia and New Zealand. The successful campaign received attention and praise from travel professionals and is credited with increasing the number of tourists to the nation within just a few years.

More Lodging Available

While the Incredible India campaign succeeded in bringing tourists to India, a lack of available lodging had to be addressed before the nation could handle a large increase in visitors. As one solution to the problem, the Ministry of Tourism has encouraged Indian entrepreneurs to start hosting tourists in bed and breakfast style guest lodging. These B&Bs offer visitors an authentic experience with Indian cuisine, culture and people, as well as an increase in the number of guest rooms available in metropolitan areas.

Transportation and Accessibility

India's crumbling infrastructure is another hurdle to the successful growth of the tourism sector. The Indian government is allocating funds to improve the infrastructure of the nation, improving access to rural areas so they become attractive to visitors. One such improvement has been the installation of heliports, where visitors can easily travel from a major metropolitan area to a rural area by helicopter.

Heritage and Ecotourism

Many visit India seeking signs of the ancient culture founded there. A popular heritage sight is the Taj Mahal, which attracts millions of visitors each year. India's Ministry of Tourism attempts to implement sustainable practices, promoting the ideals of ecotourism to its partner sites and tour guides. The Ministry also is integrating the ideals of conservation and preservation of the local ecology and culture to the greatest extent possible. The Ministry is working to create unique tourist experiences in rural India that promote local culture and have a low impact on the environment.

Health and Wellness Tourism

As the birthplace of yoga and Ayurveda, India has a particular appeal to visitors who are searching for spiritual and physical healing. Since the Beatles visited an Indian ashram in the late 1960s, the popularity of visiting these spiritual yoga centers has grown among Westerners. The Ministry uses that popularity to highlight these traditions in their campaigns.

India Tourism Development

In 2002, the Indian Ministry of Tourism launched a global marketing campaign based on the slogan "Incredible India." The ad campaign was combined with an effort to improve domestic conditions that hindered tourism, such as poor infrastructure and not enough hotels. In keeping with modern ideals, the ministry attempted to encourage sustainable practices in their growing tourism economy, preserving local ecology and culture as much as possible, and also improving the country's conference and meeting facilities.

Marketing Campaign

India has been a destination for travelers for millennia, but poor infrastructure and the lack of certain amenities have kept the tourist economy from developing further. The global marketing campaign brought India to the attention of millions of potential tourists worldwide, as the Ministry of Tourism placed print, radio and television ads in markets around the world.

Welcoming Attitudes

Complementing the Incredible India campaign abroad, the Ministry of Tourism launched a domestic campaign called, "Atithi Devo Bhavah," which means roughly "the guest is god." The ministry suggests that Indians need to embrace traditional values that have been lost, such as treating all visitors with respect, admonishing those who treat guests poorly or who deface cultural monuments. As part of the campaign, a training program aimed at the hospitality industry, including taxi drivers and tour guides, seeks to instill values in these workers such as good hygiene and behavior that is courteous, safe and maintains integrity.

Modern Tourism Practices

The Ministry of Tourism is also embracing modern tourism practices such as encouraging sustainable practices and engaging visitors in activities rather than have them serve as passive spectators. The wellness centers and yoga ashrams have drawn visitors for decades, who came to participate in and learn about ancient meditation and health techniques. More adventurous travelers seek out India's more rugged terrain to hike, bike and boat. India also draws upon the volunteer spirit of visitors from wealthier nations, who come to the country by the thousands to pitch in and improve the lives of the less fortunate.

Sustainable Practices and Ecotourism

In line with modern concerns for the environment, the Ministry of Tourism encourages sustainable practices and conservation efforts whenever possible. With a wide range of terrain, India offers adventure travelers beautiful beaches, the world's highest mountains and everything in between. With a new focus on ecotourism, tented camping has become more popular and a great way for visitors to see remote regions with little impact on the environment. For more about ecotourism in India, visit ecoindia.com.

Business Travelers

As part of the new push to make India more welcoming to visitors, India is focused on updating their meeting and conference facilities. Global hospitality companies such as the Renaissance and Marriott Hotels have opened conference facilities in large metropolitan areas such as New Delhi and Mumbai and business centers like Hydrabad. There are also large exhibition centers located around the country, such as Pragati Maidan in New Delhi, which houses shows like the International Trade Fair and the World Book Fair.

Tourism is one of the largest & important industry which is useful for the development of a nation. It occupies 11% of the world's GDP and may create 7 million new jobs by the year 2010. $595 billions have been generated by the international tourism industry in 2000.

Indian Tourism industry

Tourism in India has grown very much during the last decades. It gives the second highest net foreign exchange earnings to our economy. Foreign tourist arrivals are at 2.64 millions during 2000. Domestic tourism helps to understand various cultures and to experience national integration among the citizens

Apart from the higher class people, the middle class has emerged as a powerful source for the development of domestic tourism. Around 1.50 million domestic tourists have made a trip outside their places.

Ninth Five Year Plan

- Development of infrastructure
- Development of trekking, winter sports, wildlife and beach resorts
- Exploring new source markets in region and countries having cultural affinity
- Environmental protection and cultural preservation of national heritage projects
- Launching of national image buildings and marketing plans
- Providing inexpensive accommodation in different tourist centers
- Streaming of facilitation procedures at airports
- Human resource development
- Creating awareness
- Facilitating private sector participation in development of infrastructure

ORGANIZATIONS

1. Department of Tourism (Under the Minister of Civil Aviation & tourism)

It formulates and implements the polices and program for tourism development. It attracts foreign tourist by developing infrastructure, publicity and promotion, travel agencies, etc. It as 21 filed officers in India providing facilitation services. 18 officers are functions in overseas countries to attract tourist to India with Air India it makes joint promotional effects in US, UK, Europe, Australia and other countries.

2. India tourism development corporation (ITDC)

It is a public sector units established in 1966. It is involved in construction, management and marketing of hotels restaurants, etc. Tourist transport facilities, production, distribution and seal of tourist published materials, providing entertainment facilities, etc. are some of the services rendered by ITDC

3. Indian institution of Tourism and Travel management

It is an autonomous body to educate tourism and travel management for tourism personnel. It also organises entrepreneurship development programs, seminar, workshops, etc.

4. Institutes of Hotel Management & Catering Technology

It offers various degree/diploma courses relating to Hotel Management, nutrition, etc at various parts of the country.

5. National Institute of water sports

It is set up in Goa and conducts courses like sailing, scuba diving, water skiing, etc.

Need For Attention

The average global growth of the industry is 5% but the tourist traffic share of India is static at 0.38%.

Neighbouring countries have utilised the opportunity for their growth.

Due to the effect of Sepember 11 attack in Asia-pacific region, there was a loss of 4.4 million jobs. Also, there was 5.7% loss in tourism demands.

AWAITING OPPORTUNITIES FOR INDIA

India is Distinct in Having

- Ancient Civilization
- Natural landscape
- Traditions
- Music, dance
- Religious practices
- Exclusive festivals
- Art and Craft

Focus of the international travellor is shifting from developed regions to the developing regions.

Challenges to be Faced

- Many of the tourist site environments are unhealthy
- Facilities and services are poor in many sites
- There exists inadequate transportation to reach and continue the journey
- Infrastructure facility is very poor
- There is limited availability of tourism information at limited places
- There are regional conflicts due to which tourism is getting affected in some areas
- There is a lack of adequate security in some areas of the country which makes the tourists feel insecure

Overcoming Challenges

- ITDC have to be enriched so that it can provide adequate facilities at tourist sites like good environment, tourism information, etc.

- Present modes of transports are getting strengthened. However, the reaching tourist spots from the nearby town/city is still a dificult one. Special attention has to be paid by the Department of tourism so that its recommendation has to be implemented by the Governemnt at the earliest.
- The Central and state Governments, must have special attention and invest in large to develop the infrastructure for utilising the tourist spots.
- Tourism information must be updated often. The websites must give enriched informations with catchy phrases. Specific toll free numbers can be used for easy access of information by tourists
- The Government must take action to solve security problems and regional conflicts.
- Liberalising the visa norms can be made so that more number of tourists can arrive and stay for more days.
- Involvement of private sector in the field can be made to serve the tourists better
- Investment in HRD programmes relating to travel & tourism industry can help to promote it better
- There can be focussed promotion of various places to get attention of the travellers by using aids like short films, photographs, etc.
- Clearly planned, focussed tour packages can be introduced which may attract the travellers.

Conclusion

It is clear that there is a wide scope for underdeveloped countries like India to promote tourism. If India overcomes the challenges by enriching its present strategies, it will emerge as a best tourist spot and will yield maximum foreign exchange to our country.

Tourism Promotion Plan

In June 2006 Tasmanian Premier Paul Lennon announced that the State Government would spend $75 million on promoting Tasmanian tourism, following the withdrawal of Spirit of Tasmania III.

The plan would include $31 million of new funds, backed by $44 million already committed by Tourism Tasmania over the next four years, for marketing and promotion of the state.

The plan is designed to place the Tasmanian tourism industry in the strongest possible position for the future, with the bulk of the funding provided up front.

Following Tasmania-wide consultation, the Tourism Promotion Plan was developed and released by the Premier on 3 November 2006.

The Tourism Promotion Plan provides a number of opportunities for people working in and alongside the Tasmanian tourism industry.

The Seven TPP Programs:

Program 1 - Consumer Research

Program 2 - Spring Campaigns 07

Program 3 - Autumn/Winter Campaigns 07/08

Program 4 - Major Destination Campaign

Program 5 - Intrastate, Visiting Friends & Relatives

Program 6 - e-Marketing Platform

Program 7 - Market Ready Regional Development

Program One - Consumer Research

This program is managed by Tourism Tasmania.

The Perceptions Study

The objective of the consumer research was to better understand how both visitors to Tasmania and potential visitors to Tasmania viewed the State as a holiday destination. This was achieved by identifying the current motivational triggers and barriers associated with travelling to and around the State.

Colmar Brunton was commissioned to complete the Perceptions Study, which surveyed interstate Australians who were prepared to spend $2,000 on a holiday and Tasmanians who were prepared to spend $1,000. The project was comprehensive in its sample-size, involving 2038 interstate Australians and 525 Tasmanians.

Future research is currently being planned and will include validating the new Zone Marketing approach and review product development opportunities.

Tourism Tasmania will conduct a workshop encompassing all the initiatives from the Perceptions Study and the organisation's new strategic direction to develop a clear roadmap for the future.

Program Two - Spring Campaigns

This program involved both TT-Line and Tourism Tasmania for the 2006/07 period.

Tourism Tasmania's traditional spring campaign was extended through the use of additional media and by working cooperatively with Tourism Australia on its domestic campaigns.

This additional advertising was aligned to Tourism Tasmania's core spend, as it was in accordance with the brand look and feel of the core campaign. In addition, the media and timings were selected to complement the core campaign.

TT-Line developed and implemented three concepts.

1. The development of online advertising to enhance the Spirit of Tasmania Spring advertising campaign
2. The development, production and distribution of a 16 page full-colour North West Tasmania catalogue, and
3. The production of a 4 panel postcard and email e-card to enhance the Spirit of Tasmania Spring campaign

All three concepts were aimed at generating additional tourist numbers to visit Tasmania and in particular the north-west region.

In 2007, Tourism Tasmania developed a 32 page glossy publication called Tasmania Magazine, with stories by writers such as Leo Schofield, Neil Kearny, Mark Webber and Jo Trzcinski. The Tasmania Magazine was inserted into selected News Limited newspapers in Melbourne, Sydney, Brisbane and Adelaide on Tuesday 27th February, 2007. This represented an approximate circulation of over 1.3 million copies and achieved the impact of a quality glossy magazine with the mass reach and readership of a newspaper.

TT-Line developed the online advertising campaign "Hot Day Sale" to enhance their autumn advertising and generate additional tourist numbers to visit Tasmania.

Plans are underway for Tourism Tasmania's Autumn/Winter campaign for 2008 and the development of a new edition of the Tasmania Magazine is planned for distribution in May/June.

Program Four - Major Destination Campaign.

The findings of the major perceptions study outlined above have had an impact on the Tasmania's latest destination marketing campaign.

The February to June 2008 campaign will include media such as television, press and outdoor with an emphasis on various zones within the destination. This will help to address issues identified within the Perception Study, such as the need for greater depth of awareness of what the destination has to offer.

Program Five - Intrastate and Visiting Friends & Relatives.

The objective of the intrastate campaign was to increase awareness, knowledge and preference for Tasmania as the ideal holiday destination amongst Tasmanians.

The intrastate marketing campaign was defined by Southern Cross Television's production and broadcast of an 11 episode television series 'Discover Tasmania'. Hosted by Ed Halmagyi and Tim Campbell, the program was broadcast across Tasmania from September to December 2007.

This initiative was supported by the development of a high-quality magazine, Our Island. Two-hundred thousand copies were distributed as an insert in the Advocate, Mercury and Examiner newspapers in October 2007 into households around Tasmania. Online marketing, cooperative newspaper and television advertising campaigns, a direct marketing campaign that brought together other divisions within DTAE in the promotion of the department's Discoveries Guide and two major intrastate competitions provided longevity to the campaign which concluded in late January 2008.

The television series was so successful in attracting viewers and in increasing intrastate visitation to operator's attractions, that Southern Cross has negotiated with Channel 7 to screen the first series on mainland regional and metropolitan television. The first series will be broadcast to these markets during the next AFL season which begins at the end of April 2008 and we are currently negotiating to develop a second series of 'Discover Tasmania'.

Program Six - E-Marketing Platform

In response to fast-changing consumer trends, the e-marketing program provides for an accelerated program to implement a digital direction for Tourism Tasmania in support of industry by:

- consolidating discovertasmania.com as the primary tourism portal for all things tourism in Tasmania;
- building on Tourism Tasmania's current destinational profile by focusing on regional experiences and enhancing online information delivery and booking capabilities;

- the development of new digital content on social networking sites, for example MySpace, Facebook and YouTube;
- the delivery of value-adding information for prospects and travellers including live weather feeds and special interest video links.

Program Seven – Market Ready Regional Development

This program contained three sub-programs and was aimed at assisting the industry in product and experience development and cooperative marketing opportunities that are "market ready":

1. Regional Product and Experience Development
2. Improving the Capability of the Regional Tourism Authorities
3. Co-operative Marketing

Ministry of Tourism

The Organisation

The Ministry of Tourism, is the nodal agency for the formulation of national policies and programmes and for the co-ordination of activities of various Central Government Agencies, State Governments/UTs and the Private Sector for the development and promotion of tourism in the country.This Ministry is headed by the Union Minister for Tourism and supported by Minister of State for Tourism.

The administrative head of the Ministry is the Secretary (Tourism). The Secretary also acts as the Director General (DG) Tourism. The office of the Director General of Tourism {now merged with the office of Secretary (Tourism)} provides executive directions for the implementation of various policies and programmes. Directorate General of Tourism has a field formation of 20 offices within the country and 14 offices abroad and one sub-ordinate office/ project i.e. Indian Institute of Skiing and Mountaineering (IISM)/ Gulmarg Winter Sports Project. The overseas offices are primarily responsible for tourism promotion and marketing in their respective areas and the field offices in India are responsible for providing information service to tourists and to monitor the progress of field projects.The activities of IISM/GWSP have now been revived and various Ski and other courses are being conducted in the J&K valley.

The Ministry of Tourism has under its charge a public sector undertaking, the India Tourism Development Corporation and the following autonomous institutions:

i. Indian Institute of Tourism and Travel Management (IITTM) and National Institute of Water Sports (NIWS)

ii. National Council for Hotel Management and Catering Technology (NCHMCT) and the Institutes of Hotel Management.

Role and Functions of the Ministry of Tourism

The Ministry of Tourism functions as the nodal agency for the development of tourism in the country. It plays a crucial role in coordinating and supplementing the efforts of the State/Union Territory Governments, catalyzing private investment, strengthening promotional and marketing efforts and in providing trained manpower resources. The functions of the Ministry in this regard mainly consist of the following:

i. All Policy Matters, including:

a. Development Policies.

b. Incentives.

c. External Assistance.

d. Manpower Development.

e. Promotion & Marketing.

f. Investment Facilitation.

ii. Planning

iii Co-ordination with other Ministries, Departments, State/UT Governments.

iv Regulation:

a. Standards.

b. Guidelines.

v Infrastructure & Product Development.

a. Central Assistance.

vi. Human Resource Development

a. Institutions.

b. Setting Standards and Guidelines.

vii. Publicity & Marketing:

a. Policy.

b. Strategies.

c. Co-ordination.

d. Supervision.

viii. Research, Analysis, Monitoring and Evaluation

ix. International Co-operation and External Assistance

a. International Bodies.

b. Bilateral Agreements.

c. External Assistance.

d. Foreign Technical Collaboration

x. Legislation and Parliamentary Work

xi. Establishment matters.

xii. Vigilance matters.

xiii. Implementation of official language policy.

xiv. Budget co-ordination and related matters.

xv. Plan-coordination and monitoring.

The Functions of Attached Office viz. Directorate General of Tourism are as under [The office of DG (T) has now been merged with the office of Secretary (Tourism)]©:

i. Assistance in the formulation of policies by providing feedback from the field offices.

ii. Monitoring of Plan Projects and assisting in the Plan formulation

iii. Coordinating the activities of field offices and their supervision.

iv. Regulation:

   a. Approval and classification of hotels and restaurants.

   b. Approval of travel agents, Inbound tour operators and tourist transport operators, etc.

v. Inspection & Quality Control

   a. Guide service.

   b. Complaints and redressal.

vi. Infrastructure Development:

   a. Release of incentives.

   b. Tourist facilitation and information.

   c. Field publicity, promotion & marketing.

   d. Hospitality programmes.

   e. Conventions & conferences.

vii. Assistance for Parliamentary work.

viii. Establishment matters of Directorate General of Tourism

Tourism Policy and Schemes

In order to develop tourism in India in a systematic manner, position it as a major engine of economic growth and to harness its direct and multiplier effects for employment and poverty eradication an environmentally sustainable manner, the National Tourism Policy was formulated in the year2002.Broadly, the "Policy" attempts to:-

- Position tourism as a major engine of economic growth;
- Harness the direct and multiplier effects of tourism for employment generation, economic development and providing impetus to rural tourism;
- Focus on domestic tourism as a major driver of tourism growth.
- Position India as a global brand to take advantage of the burgeoning global travel trade and the vast untapped potential of India as a destination;
- Acknowledges the critical role of private sector with government working as a pro-active facilitator and catalyst;
- Create and develop integrated tourism circuits based on India's unique civilization, heritage, and culture in partnership with States, private sector and other agencies and
- Ensure that the tourist to India gets physically invigorated, mentally rejuvenated, culturally enriched, spiritually elevated and "feel India from within".
- Keeping is view the basic principles and guidelines of the Tourism Policy, the Ministry of Tourism has been broadly implementing the following schemes/ programs during the 11th Five Year Plan:

Guidelines for Plan Scheme(11th)

Scheme for Product/ Infrastructure Development and Destination and Circuits

Scheme of Assistance for Large Revenue Generating Projects

Scheme of Capacity Building for Service Providers (Rural Tourism)

Scheme of Rural Tourism

Guidelines for Organizing Fair & Festivals and Tourism related events

Guidelines for extending financial support for Joint Advertising in Print Media Campaign

Guidelines for production of publicity material in collaboration with Private sector

Scheme of Central Financial Assistance for Information Technology (IT) Projects

Scheme for support to Public Private Partnership in Infrastructure Development (Viability Gap undoing)

Time Share Resorts (TSR)

Marketing Development Assistance Scheme for promotion of Domestic Tourism

Revised Guidelines for Adhoc Advertisement

Scheme of Financial Assistance to the IHMs/FCIs/IITTM/ITIs/POLYTECHNIC etc

Market Research – Professional Services

National Tourism Awards

The Ministry of Tourism is running a scheme under which National Tourism Awards are given to Travel Agents and Tour Operators including best Adventure Tour Operator, best Domestic Tour Operator, most Innovative Tour Operator ,Best Mice Operator, Tourist Transport Operator, best Hotels in the different categories, Outstanding performers in Publishing, etc. Awards are also given to the meritorious students of the institutes of Hotel Management and Indian Institute of Tourism & Travel Management.

- Guidelines of National Tourism Awards for the Year 2008-09

- Awardees of National Tourism Awards for the Year 2008-09
- Awardees of National Tourism Awards for the Year 2007-08

Publicity Information Maaterial

As part of its marketing / publicity activities, the Ministry of Tourism brings out brochures, leaflets, maps, films, CDs, etc. on various topics. Each heading given below details the theme on an All-India basis based on availability of the respective products. In case of the destination folders, the leaflet / folder / brochure gives the information about the place or the destination with various facets of the facilities available, sight seeing around the place, important telephone numbers and the contact points of Indiatourism officers. Similarly, the films deal with the subject in its entirety covering all destinations of the country.

- Incredible India Theme Brochures
- Destination Leaflets
- Heritage Destination Leaflets
- Posters on different subjects & Themes
- Maps
- Films

Promotional Techniques

In order to market a product, it is necessary that information about the product reaches a prospective consumer. As applied to tourism industry, the most important function of marketing is to bring about an awareness of the product in the minds of existing as well as prospective consumer in the overall market area. All this forms a part of overall tourism promotion. The basic function of all tourism promotional activities is to have an effective and meaningful communication with the consumer and the trade intermediaries. This is possible through certain identifiable methods which are being practised by all the marketing organisations. The awareness is brought about through certain methods/marketing tools these are: (a) Advertising; (b) Public Relations.

The above tools are, however, not exclusive but complementary to each other. Proper and judicious blend of these is essential for the successful marketing of a tourism product.

Significance of Advertising

Advertising is a non-personal communication of a sales message to actual or potential purchasers of a product by a person or an organisation selling a product or a service. The sales message is delivered through a paid medium for the purpose of influencing the buying behaviour of those purchasers. The term may be defined as "any activity designed to spread information with a view to promoting the sales of marketable goods and services". As such, it operates in two ways: firstly, by spreading information among consumers, about the possibilities of consumption, and secondly, by seeking to influence their judgement in favour of the particular goods which are the subject of the advertisement. Use of certain paid media space is, however, a prerequisite. A message in the paid media must have as its purpose sale of a product or a service.

Advertising is an investment and like all investments it should produce measurable results. The first and foremost reason for setting advertising objectives is, therefore, to measure the return on one's advertising investment. The second reason is that with the availability of many alternative methods for marketing products and with customers becoming more and more value-conscious, organisations must seek the most efficient way of marketing the goods and services if they are to remain competitive.

Professor Robert Buzzell of thc Harvard Business School, gives the following example of possible advertising objectives for a consumer product advertising to increase sales directly by:

(i) Encouraging potential purchasers to visit dealers or distributors;

(ii) Announcing special sales, contests or other promotions;

(iii) Securing new dealers or distributors;

(iv) Inducing professional persons (e.g., doctors, architects) to recommend a product; and

(v) distributing coupons to be redeemed on purchases;

To create awareness and interest in the company's product by:

a. informing potential buyers about product features;

b. announcing the availability of new products;

c. demonstrating the benefits of a products use;

d. comparing a product with competing product;

e. showing how a product should be used;

f. informing potential buyers about the company's technical skills, production facilities, technical services, etc.;

g. informing purchasers about where products can be obtained;

h. announcing changes in prices, packages, labels, etc.; and

j. publicising a new brand name or symbol.

The above advertising objectives for the manufacturer's consumer product advertising can be applied or the tourism product advertising to achieve the best possible results. The broad objectives in tourism advertising include making the tourist product as widely known as possible and making it as attractive as possible for the prospective consumers.

Selection of Media

The selection of the medium or media will depend upon the factors like the area to be covered, the type of audience to be reached, the appeals to be made and upon the services and facilities of the particular medium in relation to costs. The important factors which influence the media selection are: (i) media habits of the target audience; (ii) product characteristics: for example, TV may be the appropriate media for those products which may require a demonstration of their operation for effective impact on the target audience; and (iii) cost of the media.

Selection of Message

The message selected should be such that it retains the interest in the minds of the customer about the product. The customer must maintain his interest in the message, and secure the action desired by the seller of the product. The objective is to present the advertiser's message in such a way that the illustration may lead the reader to favourable consideration of the advertisement. The important characteristics of an effective messag are:

(i) *Information:* it should be adequate for a decision,

(ii) *Interest:* it should be able to catch the attention of the largest audience,

(iii) *Authenticity:* it should avoid exaggerated claims,

(iv) *Persuasion:* it should be capable of creating a favourable conviction in the target audience, and

(v) *Memory value:* it should have something in it which can help the target audience to remember it.

Factor of Costing

The agency must relate the estimated cost and the results expected from advertising. Can the advertiser carry on a campaign large enough to make it effective? Are the funds available or will they become available through the sale of the product? How much does the agency spend for the advertising? The various methods commonly used are:

(i) *Affordable method:* here, the advertising budget is set on the basis of what the agency can afford;

(ii) *Percentage of sales method:* in this case, the agency sets the advertising budget on the basis of specific percentage of sales;

(iii) *Competitive parity method:* here the company sets its budget to match those of its major competitors;

(iv) *Objective and task method:* in this the advertising budget represents the outlay required to perform the various tasks which are necessary to achieve the properly defined advertising objectives of the company. This method is considered the most rational.

Advertising Evaluation

It is very important for the agency to ensure that the money spent on advertisement does bring returns by way of increased sales. This could be done by way of evaluating or testing the effectiveness of advertising. Test may be applied before advertisement has been run. Pre-testing of an advertisement prevents expenditure that would not be profitable and leads to expenditure that give the best results. In determining advertising effectiveness the commonly used methods are:

Coupon Response: Answer-back coupons, with some inducement, are incorporated in many advertisements. The amount of response is an indication of the effectiveness of the concerned advertisement.

Recall Tests: Here the respondents are shown the magazine cover or any other media vehicle in which the concerned advertisement had appeared. They are then asked to tell which advertisements in that publication they remember.

Recognition Tests : Here the respondents are shown the advertisement and asked if they have read them.

Sales Tests: Here, the actual sales results before and after the concerned advertising are examined. The sales results in the selected 'test markets' are also compared to those in some chosen 'control markets', i.e., the markets where the concerned advertising is not done. In the field of tourism, advertising is mainly used to create initial awareness and interest in the tourist service or destination to be promoted and motivates potential tourists to decide to make further enquiries about costs, bookings, facilities, etc. It implies indirect communication with selected target groups—the potential tourist—through paid messages designed to promote a particular destination or an area. For a country which is trying to attract tourists, there can be two forms of advertising: (i) consumer advertising, and (ii) trade advertising. To reach a wide a number of consumers, such media as newspapers, radio spots, TV prime time are used. However, this form of advertisement is very expensive. It is extremely difficult to afford such a type of advertisement because of financial constraints. Trade advertising on the hand is an indirect form of advertising and is less expensive.

In marketing a tourist product advertising plays a very important role. If the right combination of conditions is present the effect of advertising would be to increase the demand for the particular country's tourist product. Among the factors favourable to the successful use of advertising are the rising trend of demand in the particular product and an opportunity to stimulate selective demand, i.e., preference for the particular product. This is most likely where there is a possibility of product differentials, and where consumer satisfaction depends largely on hidden qualities that cannot easily be judged at the time of purchase, or where strong emotional buying motive exists as in the case of tourism.

Public Relations is the "art and science of planning and implementing honest, two-way communication and understanding between a company or an organisation and the many different groups with which it is concerned in the course of its operation." It is also defined as "continuous and consistent representation of an organisation's policies to the public at large to sections of the public who have a special interest in the organisation's activities, e.g., to various strata of employees, shareholders, actual and potential customers as well as its local and national governments. *Public Relations News*, a weekly newsletter written for the PR profession in the United States of America, defines PR as "a management function that evaluates public attitudes, identifies the policies and procedures of an individual or an organisation as they affect the public interest, and executes a programme of action to earn public understanding and acceptance." The internationally accepted definition of PR however is that it is "the deliberate, planned and sustained effort to establish and maintain mutual understanding between an organisation and its public." The main function of public relations is to inform the public about the activities of an organisation. In other words, it is a part of an organisation's total communication effort.

THE SOCIETY FOR PROMOTION OF TOURISM

The Society for Promotion of Nature Tourism and Sports (SPORTS) is a society formed by the Lakshadweep Administration in 1982 with the avowed aim of tapping tourism potential of the islands and to act as the nodal agency of Lakshadweep Administration for promotion of tourism in the islands. It is registered under Section 3 of the Societies Registration Act of 1860. Hon'ble Administrator, Lakshadweep is the Chairman of the Society and Shri. J.K.DADOO IAS is the Chairman at present. Under him Managing Director discharges the functions of Chief Executive Officer.

The primary aim of the organization is to promote eco-friendly tourism and recreational activities in the islands in association with and under guidance of the Lakshadweep Administration. SPORTS also acts as hospitality and catering wing of the Lakshadweep Administration. The Society operates tourist resorts at Kadmat, Minicoy and Kavaratti. It also conducts package tour covering three islands - Minicoy, Kalpeni and Kavaratti. Apart from operating these resorts SPORTS is manning State Guest House and Dak Bungalows of the Administration. SPORTS also strives to provide employment opportunities to the educated locals the tourism sector.

The holiday packages drawn up by SPORTS, while providing the tourist with a memorable experience, protect the environment and do not upset the delicate balance between man and nature. In recognition of the Lakshadweep Administration's policy and the projects of the SPORTS that helped to preserve the ecology of the island

and create environmental awareness while promoting tourism, SPORTS has been awarded the 'most eco-friendly organisation' award of the Union Ministry of Tourism for the year 1996-97. Due to dedicated efforts of the SPORTS Lakshadweep islands have gained popularity as a unique tourist destination and as a haven for nature lovers. SPORTS is gearing up to diversify in to what can be termed as fishery tourism wherein marine and fishery resources around the islands will be woven in to tourism. Rich secular and cultural heritage of the islands rarely seen elsewhere in the country will also be promoted.

2

MARKET ANALYSIS FOR TOURISM PROMOTION

Having understood the current profile of Indian tourism, it is possible to analyse the marketing efforts put in by the Department of Tourism, Government of India. While starting tourism promotion in a modest way in the early fifties, the Government of India had no clear-cut objectives and goals about how to go about it. Tourism promotion was considered an information service like information on any other aspect of a country i.e. trade, economy, etc. Nothing more.

To most government officials involved in tourism promotion in the early fifties, international tourism meant that some affluent people from rich countries with a lot of money and some curiosity (especially from the US) were willing to travel to foreign lands. It was recognised that the first preference of such people in North America would be Europe which they considered the cradle of Western civilisation. However, the retired and more affluent among them could be persuaded to take round-the-world trips either by ship or by air which sometimes included India. That was the India's target group in the fifties and sixties.

In North America, or for that matter in the entire Western world, India, if known at all, at that time had the image primarily of an exotic country — hot and humid, poor and backward, a land of snake charmers and rope walkers — an image which the British authors like Kipling had built up over the decades. The British rulers projected this image as they had to stand the heat of long summers in India to administer the country. Their families retired to the hills with cooks, bearers, nannies and gardeners and there was little attempt at meeting the people of India and understanding their rich culture.

In the early fifties, the government decided that India should have overseas offices to project a new image of the country as a tourist destination. The markets chosen were the USA, the UK followed by West Germany, France and Australia. These offices were essentially information offices whose job was to distribute and disseminate tourist information through brochures printed in India. In an effort to do everything in India, they forgot that their publicity material exported out of India was not attractive enough and of the best quality.

Although these offices were useful in projecting the new image of an independent India, some of the offices were perhaps opened a little too soon. For instance, an India tourist office was opened in Germany in 1957 at a time when the Germans had just undertaken travelling outside their country. They were not ready for India. It took them a decade before they began taking long distance holiday trips to countries like India and that too only when holidays to India became relatively inexpensive due to the introduction of charters and the cheaper inclusive group fares on scheduled carriers. Similarly, India opened a tourist office in Japan in 1964, when Japan first liberalised its foreign exchange restrictions and allowed the Japanese to take only three hundred dollars for travel overseas. But traffic from Japan to India remained static for five years as the Japanese did not think beyond the USA and Europe as their preferred holiday or business destinations. In Australia also, the story was more or less repeated as Australians started taking India holidays or stopovers on the way to Europe only in the early seventies. However, these tourist offices were useful in paving the way for tourism from these markets in later decades.

Modest advertising campaigns were launched by the tourist offices overseas within their limited resources. It was generally a well thought out activity undertaken on the advice of the professional advertising agencies hired by each tourist office locally to improve the image of India as a land of Ajanta-Ellora, the Taj Mahal, the Himalayas and Mahabalipuram. Cultural tourism relating to monuments and an ancient civilisation was the initial thrust of promotion as people in the Western world could more readily identify India with such an image. The frequency and the size of advertisements was inadequate. Advertisements were released mostly in black and white as colour advertising was considered too expensive. At the same time, tourist offices, however, established contacts with the tour-operators and travel agents to persuade them to send their clients to India.

Well Planned Marketing

Market planning in the fifties and the sixties was not really feasible because the base of Indian tourism was narrow. The resources for promotion were even more limited and, tourism being a new industry, personnel were not well-trained.

For preparing any successful marketing plan, we deal with four variables, popularly known in the marketing jargon as the four Ps.

Product: It means attractions or tourist resources that a country can offer — beautiful monuments, scenic beauty, beach and mountain resorts, transportation services, good hotel accommodation, polite and friendly people, etc.

Price: It implies the optimal rates at which the tourism product (holiday) can be sold.

Place: Most suitable distribution channels. In other words, the markets where the product should be sold and the network through which it is sold.

Promotion: It implies the communication process, public relations, advertising, promotion, etc.

To begin with, the Indian tourist 'product' had several drawbacks. The major shortcoming was the image. India did not enjoy the image of a holiday destination.

Indians were often shocked to see the results of surveys conducted by organisations like PATA showing India in a terribly bad light. Despite the shock the fact remained that India had an image problem about its tourist product everywhere, especially in the USA. The picture in Western Europe was not very different. In 1961, the London Observer questioned its readers where they were planning to spend their holidays in 1962. India was not even mentioned among the first twelve popular destinations. A member of the Indian Parliament on return from England in 1966 quoted a placard shown in London which read:

Positive news came from Germany. In a survey carried out in the Federal Republic of Germany, the respondents were asked in the early sixties: 'If you could do as you liked, where would you go and what would you like to see and do most of all'? They were given the choice of twenty two places and activities; for example:

The Egyptian Pyramids

The ruins of ancient Greece

The skyscrapers of New York

The Kremlin in Moscow

The Hollywood film studios

A journey across the ocean in a sailing ship

To watch a nuclear explosion

The Isle of Capri

Paris

St. Peter's in Rome

Tour to India

Surprisingly, India was the most popular country outside the European continent.

The image problem was further complicated by the inadequacy of transport and hotel accommodation, both in quality and quantity. In 1967, the Director of the Government of India tourist office in San Francisco called on a major travel agency and the following conversation took place with the President of the company, with the President doing the most of the talking.

"Sir you have beautiful, colourful literature on India. I must compliment you on its production."

"Thank you very much. How is the business?"

"You have a great country with varied tourist attractions."

"Thank you again for saying that."

"You have a very nicely located office in a central place in San Francisco. Your staff is polite and efficient."

"Well you are making my day...."

"But, Sir, why don't you close down your office?"

"Now, tell me, why do you say that after paying me all these compliments this morning?"

"Better buy some planes for Indian Airlines for tourists. I cannot get confirmation on Indian Airlines for my clients for months. How can I sell India?" he asked. "Presently, what you need is capacity on Indian Airlines and not promotion. Close your shop and go back home," he advised.

This was duly reported to the Government of India, but the government had its own priorities. It was a time when Indian Airlines had not bought its Boeings and Airbuses, and the capacity on most routes was limited.

No amount of marketing and promotion could help India with these constraints.

The Indian Airlines' capacity was increased in December 1970 when Boeing 737s were bought; later their fleet was augmented by the addition of more such planes and in 1988 and after by the purchase of 19 Airbuses. Despite these purchases, Indian Airlines' capacity did not catch up with the increasing demand. The situation is a little better today though popular tourist routes are still overcrowded during the season. By 1997, the Indian Airlines had more planes than pilots, and Indian Airlines fleet was underutilised—the other extreme.

The introduction of a Hotel Loan Development Fund in 1968 eased the accommodation situation somewhat. While marketing India's tourist product, price too was an important factor to be taken into consideration. Although India's tourist facilities were relatively inexpensive, the high airfares were a negative factor in the major tourist markets of the world. The majority of tourists to India come by air from long distances — an expensive way of travelling compared to road or rail travel as in Europe.

It would be seen that India's share in world tourism cannot be very large till there is a significant inter-regional movement. If the experience of other countries provides a clue, large-scale tourism cannot originate from long-distance markets. European countries and Canada, Mexico and the Carribbean receive a majority of their tourists from the neighbouring areas. East Asia — Thailand, Singapore, Hong Kong, the Philippines and Malaysia — receives a sizeable number of visitors from neighbouring countries. Till such time as India develops large-scale inter-regional traffic, it cannot have "mass tourism" or even tourism on a large-scale. Tense political relations and economic weaknesses of India's neighbours preclude any such possibility in the coming years.

Keeping in mind these factors, Indian advertising strategy in the sixties was essentially to tell American travellers they could break their journey in India on round-the-world tours, and to the Europeans that India was a home of a great civilisation, culture and architectural wonders. A market study conducted in the United States through the Stanford Research Institute in the early sixties revealed that Americans having an annual income of US $ 10,000 to 15,000 per year alone could afford to travel to India and in addition, only those who had a lot of intellectual curiosity. Indian advertising was, therefore, targeted to the people in this income bracket and among them also to those who had already travelled to Europe. (Now, the target group is with annual income of US$ 50,000) The headline of an advertisement released by the Government of India Tourist Office in New York in the mid-sixties read:

The Communication

The text of one advertisement told the readers about the great attractions of Europe but advised them to see India if they had already seen Europe and wanted to see something more interesting and different. Till the end of the sixties, India's tourism promotional campaign was in response to the existing market conditions — a low profile approach to the rich and educated segment of the population.

Well Structured Planning

It was only in 1967 that a separate Ministry of Tourism and Civil Aviation was created under a cabinet minister. Tourism, Civil Aviation and the various corporations relating to these activities came under the charge of this ministry. The results were amazing, and for the first time an integrated marketing plan was developed. Air India joined hands with the Department of Tourism in active promotion of India as a tourist destination. A new scheme called "Operation Europe" was launched in 1968 in Europe to, market Indian tourism. Air India not only made financial contributions to the promotional budget of the tourist offices, but also allotted targets to their field offices in Europe to sell Indian tourism. More tourist offices were opened in Europe as a result of this scheme. The tourist officers became "market oriented" and they started travelling extensively to meet tour-operators selling India in major markets. The scheme was considered successful and was later extended to all parts of the world. Indian Airlines, which had not actively advertised overseas, also joined by allocating a modest budget for overseas promotion through travel trade press.

The new advertising strategy had an element of aggressive selling. Price became an important element in the advertising text to draw customers to India. The idea was to dispel the misgiving that the prices of Indian tours must be high and not within the reach of most people. An attempt was made to project India as a destination by itself and affordable too. Given below are some of the headlines of the advertisements released in 1967 and after:

The Taj Mahal is in India it is not India : The objective was to inform people about many attractions of India other than the Taj in the great subcontinent of India. A similar approach was directed towards trade advertising. An advertisement in 1968 said:

Ten Wonders of India Check the ones your Clients have Missed : The text described the ten wonders of India as Ajanta-Ellora, the Shaking Minarets of Ahmedabad, Khajuraho, Gir Lion Sanctuary, Tiger Shikar (it was not banned at that time), Sun Temple of Konarak, Kashmir, Cochin, Darjeeling and Goa.

Price, as mentioned earlier, became an important factor in Indian advertising from 1969 onwards. Special excursion and group fares had been introduced from USA and Europe which made Indian tourist packages attractive and competitive. For instance, India could offer package tours from Japan to India cheaper than the European and US tour packages. In Europe, India started marketing inexpensive tours at almost the price of charter tours. In 1969, an advertisement in the USA proclaimed:

India Give-Away 17 Days $ 799 The Text Ran : "If you thought a holiday in India was an expensive affair, we would like to give you a surprise."

A year later, India was publicising tours ranging from $ 654 for seventeen days to $ 1,757 for twenty-five days including Nepal and Sikkim. The above theme was adopted to meet the changing requirements of the new class of visitors—the budget conscious travellers. Tourist offices kept a list of tours marketed by various tour-operators abroad with departure dates. These lists were mailed to people who wrote to tourist offices for information. The idea was to support the marketing efforts of tour operators and to enable the potential tourist to make a quick decision in the choice of his holiday. A favourable climate for India was developing as far as tourism was concerned.

However, the old theme was not forgotten Expo'70 was held in Tokyo in 1970. To take advantage of the flow of traffic to Japan because of this trade fair, the India tourist office ran the following advertisement in the USA:

After Expo'70 and before Europe see India : The Government of India tourist office in Tokyo followed up this theme by opening a tourist information booth in the Indian pavilion at Expo'70 and distributed millions of pieces of tourism literature in Japanese and other languages.

India carried out a market survey in 1961-62, 1964-65 followed by 1972-73 on the behavioural pattern of foreign tourist traffic. The survey revealed that destination traffic to India had risen from 43.2 per cent in 1961 to 73.6 per cent in 1972-73 and the indications were that more people would come to India for a destinational holiday if right conditions were created. The market planners in India re-oriented their thinking on promotion towards developing the Indian tourist product with a new focus on beach and mountain resorts, supported by cultural tourism which is in abundance all over India. Air India helped by establishing promotional air fares through IATA from several tourist generating markets taking multi-stopover requirements into account.

Europe/India GIT had relatively a low discount of thirty four per cent, but this was because high proration was involved on domestic sectors. For instance, the GIT fare for routing Paris-Mumbai-Delhi-Srinagar-Varanasi-Kathmandu-Patna-Calcutta-Madras-Trivandrum-Cochin-Bangalore-Hyderabad-Mumbai-Paris cost F.Fr. 4,670 in 1976 of which the international carrier was eventually left with F.Fr. 2,447 for the Paris-Bombay-Paris sector. Simultaneously, separate promotional fares were established allowing higher discount of fifty seven per cent on point-to-point journey for Europe-India GIT, since the proration was nil.

In 1983, there was a free for all battle of airfares in European countries. In order to corner a larger share of the market, most airlines offered discounted fares. So the tourist traffic to India did not decline from Europe in spite of the overall recession. Europeans preferred India at that time over destinations like Hong Kong, Thailand and Singapore.

Taking advantage of stopover facilities under long distance IATA fares, the Government of India tourist office in Tokyo ran an advertisement all over East Asia with those headlines.

India's Nine Cities are Included Free in your Ticket to Europe/USA : The text told the travellers that they could easily break journey in India as no extra fare was involved and that land arrangements could be made for ten to twenty five dollars a day depending upon one's requirements. The advertisement was so effective that a number of foreign carriers complained to the India tourist office that their workload had increased as making tickets with too many stopovers was not only a complicated job but also a risky one for them, as they could lose their clients to a competing airline.

With a little more confidence in selling India, the tourist offices settled down to diversify their product by spreading more extensive knowledge of India's tourist attractions. The theme changed to the variety that was India. A concerted drive was made to move traffic from the traditional golden triangle of Delhi-Agra-Jaipur to Kashmir in the North, and Southern and Eastern India. A study conducted in the USA in 1974 through the Opinion Research Corporation of USA regarding the new profile of the visitor to India summed up the profile of the potential American travellers to India in the following words:

Historically, travellers to India have come mainly from an elite group — people of wealth, with time for extensive travel, and often from the older age brackets or retired. A further distinguishing characteristic of this traditional, "quality" source of visitors has been relatively high frequency of foreign travel. Quite logically, frequent travellers are good prospects for India because they have been to a number of countries and are ready to see another one. This research confirmed the importance of the frequent traveller as good potential for India. There is every reason to continue to woo him/her through travel agents, advertising and other appropriate means.

Indian research identified another important group, perhaps not too well recognised hitherto — young travellers (18-29 years age group). While continuing to market Indian travel aggressively to the older market of frequent travellers, Indian tourism may well wish to direct additional marketing effort to the young potential group.

The newer potential group — young travellers — are a large group of prospects, relatively affluent, interested in India, and compatible in their thinking with the things India offers and requires of its visitors.

To broad base the market on the basis of identification of potential American travellers, the Indian tourist office in the USA, ran the diary of a traveller to India who tells his experience in the form of a series of advertisements.

3

PRINCIPLES OF TOURISM MARKETING

Marketing is a human activity. All the activities of tourism marketing bear a glaring testimony to this fact. In tourism marketing, we deal with mobile, enthusiastic and pleasure-seeking humans. They are on travel sprees. They want to enjoy the nice places of the world! They are efficient (at least during the courses of their journeys), conscious of the environs they visit, always careful about the money they spend, keen to explore and receptive to every phenomenon/ product/service that makes comfortable or ecstatic.

We have defined Marketing in this chapter. Let us now define the term Tourism Marketing. According to Krippendorf, "Marketing in tourism is to be understood as the, systematic and co-ordinated execution of business policy by a tourist undertaking, whether private_ or State, owned at local, regional, national and international levels, to achieve the optimal satisfaction of the needs of identifiable consumer groups and in doing so, achieves an appropriate return."

According to Burkart and Medlick, "Tourism marketing activities are systematic and coordinated efforts extended by the National Tourist Organisation and/or tourists at local levels to optimise the satisfaction of tourist groups and individuals in view of sustained tourism growth."

According to A Kumar, "Tourism marketing is the delineation and execution of activities related to tourism their professional planning and execution and finally, ensuring the satisfaction of customers (tourists) in such a manner that the marketing objectives of the tourism organisation are achieved within the framework of social, economic, political and environmental components of the place/region/country of origin as well as that of the place/region/country of tour destination."

Thus, we can arrive at some conclusions regarding tourism marketing, as follows :-

(A) Tourism marketing is the process of delivering satisfaction to tourists and in this process, the tourism marketer achieve his personal goals or the goals of the firm he works for.

(B) Tourism marketing is a service-based activity. Some parts of its realm are products, some of them (like food beverages etc.) being very important.

(C) Just like other types of marketing, tourism marketing also involves:

Strategic Planning (which includes definition of business mission, corporate strategic planning, business strategic planning, goal formulation definition of a marketing plan, finalization of marketing programmes, implementation of marketing programmes and finally, receipt of feedback and control);

Analysis of Marketing Opportunities (which includes marketing research, study of marketing environment, study of consumer behaviour and finally, study of competition);

Selection of Targeted Markets (which includes forecasting market demand, defining market segments, making plans for market targeting and finally, product positioning);

Design of Appropriate Marketing Strategies (which includes definition and identification of market leaders, challengers, followers and niches, defining the PLC of the product and using this knowledge to create market niches for the product/service and finally, understanding the intricacies of import and export management);

Planning Marketing Programmes (which includes definition and management of product lines and brands, development and testing of new products, brand management, marketing of services, pricing policies and discounts, definition and consolidation of marketing channels, study and consolidation of physical distribution channels, making effective promotion strategies, defining sales promotion and public relations programmes and finally, management of the sales force);

Implementing Marketing Programmes (which includes study/creation of a marketing organisation and implementation of marketing programmes in targeted market niches); and.

Controlling (which includes various types of control systems in the parlance of marketing).

(1) It is a process of transforming potential customers (tourists) into actual customers.

(2) It is a fine technique for generating and consolidating tourism demand.

(3) It can be used to increase market share of the tourism marketer.

(4) It essentially uses the tenets of communication, business management and psychology to win the markets in the parlance of tourism administration.

(5) It deals with human beings most of the times; they are the customers with very special and weird needs. Most of them indulge in activities related to tourism due to the fact that they want to enjoy. This peculiar feature of tourism marketing makes it special. It also demands different marketing strategies to woo the customers towards the products and services that are offered to them.

(6) Tourism packages, Group inclusive Tours, economy package deals and luxury packages area part of the gamut of tourism marketing.

(7) It involves many services or products of the infrastructure of a region or country. This makes it a Herculean effort; without making right types of teams, a tourism marketer cannot succeed in this effort.

(8) Tourism marketing starts from implementation of local or regional programmes but eventually, all the marketers try (or dream) to win international market hitches which were hitherto beyond their reach.

Tourism is predominantly a service. It involves many people (tourists, tour operators, transporters, hotel staff, guides, restaurant staff, disk jockeys etc.). It is of perishable nature.

The unique features of tourism demand are as follows :-

(a) It is perishable by nature.

(b) The demand is more during peak seasons and very low during off seasons.

(c) Tourists demand products and services of different kinds from the producers of the same set of tourism services or products. But they have to produce all such types of these services or product to remain competitive in the markets.

(d) Demand for luxury products and services is low. Demand for low-end services and product is very high.

(e) Some tourists, who may be belonging to middle-income strata of the society, may try to touch, albeit occasionally, the luxury norms of the strata that are above their strata.

(f) For some tourist spots, the demand is more or less inelastic. But for others, it is elastic.

As already stated, tourism is a service. It comprises some products as well. These include food, liquor, beverages, gifts, souvenirs, items, of daily use etc. But basically, the tourist (customer) buys services while he takes up a tour or itinerary. Example: One cannot expect a tourist to go to Mauritius to buy a few items that are typical to that country. He travels to that country to enjoy her environs, swim in the blue waters of the ocean, stay at exotic places and have a glimpse of the coral reefs that are under the waters of the ocean. He may or may not buy gifts or souvenirs, though he would certainly eat the cuisine of Mauritius.

Now that we are clear about the tenet that tourism is a service, we would have to weave a strategy set to bring customers to our fold. Service marketing is different from product marketing. It is intangible; the tourist cannot consume a tourist spot can only enjoy its environs. When he goes back to his native place, he takes sweet memories along with him. The tourism product is, therefore, essentially associated with 3 features, as follows: -

(A) Perceptions in the mind of the tourist-to-be about the tourist spot, including his expectations and a portrayal of what is in store for him.

(B) The actual experiences (good or bad) of the tourist at the spot.

(C) Sweet memories (even bitter ones) that he takes back along with him to his native place.

If a customer tries a product and does not like it, he discards it. But if a tourist tries a tourist spot and does not like it, he cannot cancel his tour. This feature differentiates tourism (as a service) from other services and products. He cannot call it a day in the middle of the journey because he was offered beef and pork by the hotel! He has to drag on somehow. Our advice to the tourism marketer is-do not let the tourist have the feeling of dragging on; eliminate this feeling as soon as it develops in his mind. If you don't, he would not give a good word-of-mouth about your tourist spot or service to others. You would lose him as well as scores of other tourists who could have become your customers, had he been treated nicely to kill that feeling of dragging on.

Further, tourism, as a service, is given only when political stability of the region is ensured.

Instance: Kashmir is a paradise on the earth but not a hot spot for tourists because of the supremacy of terrorists in that valley. A tourist does not like the hullabaloo of crowd, rallies, riots, arson and instability. He wants to enjoy and relax at the tourist spot; he may have spent the savings of his return to undertake the trip. Every tourism organisation must understand this fact.

Salient Features

The following features are important :—

(a) Tourism marketing activities are executed at regional, national and international levels.

(b) It leads to creation of a service or set of services. Some products are also included in its gamut but the "service aspect" of this gargantuan field is more important.

(c) It is a managerial process and is designed to earn profits for the tourism marketing firm or the producer who manufactures products/services related to tourism.

(d) The basic tenet of tourism marketing is the satisfaction of needs of tourists (or would-be tourists).

(e) New products/services can be created and marketed from a scratch and also, old products/ services can be marketed/sold to customers.

(f) The nature of tourism product/service is perishable. Hence, tourism marketers are always on their toes to market these products/services to the prospective buyers so that marketers are able to sell as much of these within the given time frames.

(g) Just like they try to do in other marketing programmes, tourism marketers try to create new users, convert light users into medium users and convert medium users into heavy users.

(h) Links of tourism marketers are at regional, national and global levels. They cannot survive in the markets without associating with their counterparts in other regions of the world. They have to depend, unlike conventional marketers, on such persons or firms for ensuring that their clients (tourists) get the coveted sets of products/services. Thus, distribution of the product or service is done by many players, each one of them claiming a small share in the profit cake. In conventional marketing, the distribution channels take a share of profits after the sale has been effected. In tourism marketing, various components of tourism get their respective shares in advance. Example: The airline, hotel, local transporter etc. get their amounts in advance. Shopping is done by the tourist either through a credit card or by paying cash at the counter. Other hotel expenses like bar, restaurant are paid for by the tourist when he checks out of the hotel. In some cases, tickets to various forts, palaces, parks etc. are to be purchased by the tourist at such spots. Hence, some components of the itinerary are prepaid while some other have to be paid for at the time of purchasing those components. Thus, the system of extending credit does not exist in tourism marketing, especially in international tourism marketing. There are 3 exceptions to this rule. Firstly, in the operations of time share resorts, tourists-to-be because members and use the tourist spot for a limited number of days. They pay some amount in advance and pay the balance in convenient installments. Secondly, some tourists may take loans from banks and private lenders and pay back to them after they have completed the tours. In the second case, the payments are made to tour operators in advance. Thirdly, some tour operators have also started extending credit facilities to tourists; they charge interest and deliver services related to transport, accommodation and leisure before actually receiving the payments. However in general, the tourism industry is the "first pay avail later" type of industry.

(i) Tourists have to be guided throughout the course of an itinerary. That is because they' are new to the tourist spot. Language, cultural differences and individual motivation are some of the factors that affect their actions and desires lour guides, hotel staff, transporters and operative staff at fun parks, theme parks and other places of leisure help these tourists so that they could enjoy their stints at such places. So, tourism marketing does not end with sale of tickets or booking of hotel rooms. It must be executed in a professional manner till the last phase of the tour itinerary.

(j) As already stated, differences in life-styles, languages, cultures, cuisine, daily habits religions and perceptions (of tourists) force marketers to adopt varying strategies during the course of an itinerary. Each one of tourists ought to be looked after in a different manner. In the parlance of Group Inclusive Tours (GITs), individual attention cannot be given. But in individual and family tours, the needs of an individual or a family can be addressed with professional finesse. However, GITs are cheap and individual/family tours (or those that are organised according to special programmers) are very costly.

(k) Production and consumption of tourism services are closely interrelated. Most of the tourism services cannot be consumed incrementally. So, consumption, once started, cannot be stopped are modified. So, risk or uncertainty is higher for the customer. So, he seeks precise information sets or data before he undertakes a tour. He cannot see, feel, touch or inspect the services/products related to tourism before he decides to use them. But he can make comparisons of services offered by different competitors, namely, resorts, airlines, hotels, bars, discotheques etc. But here lies the crux of the problem. He does not know much (or anything) about the tourist place he intends to visit. He can only use a few criteria, namely, grade of the hotel, location of the hotel, class of airline (executive, royal executive, economy etc.), duration of the tour, reputation of the travel agency and image of the tourist spot! country, to take a decision.

When he actually goes through the tour, then only he realises what were the wrong decisions in his selection.

(l) Different manufacturers join hands to form a tourism product. An airline considers seats flown or passenger miles covered as its product. A hotel produces guest nights. A theatre considers the number of visitors as its product. All these components form a whole that we call Tourism Product. As already stated, services form a major part of this product. Marketing efforts are needed not only to sell all these components as a whole, but also to execute these components when the tourist places an order to buy the package. Once an order has been placed (and money received), neither the buyer nor the seller can withdraw from the contract. Products and services cannot be rejected in tourism. However, these can be modified (at a cost to the customer) but within the limits imposed by the itinerary, various producers of products and services, law of the land and financial resources of the customer (tourist).

(m) Tourism demand is unstable. It depends upon seasons political upheavals, wars, modes of transport, accessibility to the tourist spot, financial resources of the customer (tourist), currency fluctuations, international relations force *mejeure'* etc.

(n) Travel motivations are diverse in nature. Different people take up tours for different reasons.

Instance: For the youth, fun could be the criterion to visit London. But for an old couple, ancient monuments, the Big Ben and Stonehenge could be the places to be visited (and not fun parks and night life). Humans are different in terms of motivations, perceptions and actions. So, they ought to be treated as individuals. Tour programmers are costly. Individual tour programmes are much more costlier than GITs. The marketer must, therefore, identify some common motivations of the tourist group. He should segregate customers on the basis of these travel motivations. It would be easier for him to understand their precise needs and serve them.

PRINCIPLES

Marketing is essentially a human activity. It is a social science. The ultimate objective of a marketer is to develop an image in the minds of the target customers, which should enable them to buy your products and services for long periods of time. The products, services and methodologies for delivering them take a back-seat; what remains vital for the success of a business is the development and maintenance of healthy relationships with the targeted market niches. And that is not at all a difficult task if the firm in question completes its homework before undertaking actions to win its markets. Let us begin with some basic terms.

Human Beings : An individual is a human being who lives in the world according to the laws defined by nature. Humans are individuals but they are social beings as well, just like any other living species. Human beings are living, perceiving forms of life. They respond to stimuli of five types-vision, sound, touch, taste and smell. Humans are also keen to survive and grow. For many of them, however, growth in mental terms is more important than survival.

The Needs and Wants : A need is the state of felt deprivation of some basic satisfaction in an individual. Every human being has some needs. These needs vary from individual to individual. If, for example, a person is hungry, then food is his need. Hunger is a physiological process.

Food would safety hunger of the individual. We are marketing our products, services and thoughts to humans. Every human being has set of needs.

The need set of every person varies but we can classify the same, for our convenience, into 5 broad categories. This classification was given by Henry Maslow. It is as follows:-

Basic : These are the physiological needs, like food, clothing, sex, shelter and other vital requirements for survival. These needs arise because of the very existence of man and he ought to satisfy them in order to thrive on this planet. Example: A young boy needs food immediately after his return from his school.

Security : These are the needs to be satisfied after the basic needs have been satisfied. These include the security of home, family and belongings. Every person wants to operate in a stable and terror—free environment. He wants to lie without any threats to his existence. The basic needs are satisfied easily (even by the poorest of people) but security needs demand more resource and physical efforts. Example: A person would like to keep his home secure by locking its main entrance, lest a thief should break into his house and take away his valuables, or harm his family members.

Social : Man is a social animal. He wants to move in the company of those people who are dear to him. Naturally, he would seek to be a part of only those groups in which, he is heard, valued and cared for. However, some people may not have social needs at all; they might love to remain in the secluded corners of their homes or offices. In general, however, man expects to remain in a pleasant company. Example: An elder person may not like to go home for most of the time and remain in the temple where he prays. At home, he might be feeling out of place as nobody might be giving ample time (and attention) that may be due to him. The company of his friends (who are mostly elders of his age group) might be a blessing for him.

Ego : Every person has an ego set. If his ego set is offended, he retaliates (through words, gestures or even through physical actions). He takes pride in some activities and would like to be known because of them. Ego is an essential ingredient of man and he cannot be told to shun it. Self-esteem is a part of this set of needs. The meaning of both these terms is similar, with only a few minor variations. Example: An executive could have ego due to the fact that he has been authorised to purchase goods worth *US$ 27,000* for his firm.

Self-Actualisation : Every human being is a minute representation of the Almighty. God has sent him to this mortal world for carrying out some tasks. However, some tasks are related to the benefit of the mankind. Every person may not have an inkling of the needs of people and environment around him. A person with an activated self-actualisation need becomes a great person during his lifetime. He forgets about his basic needs and works for the masses. Examples: Gandhi, Martin Luther King, Mother Teresa etc.

The needs of people vary and most of them continue to struggle for satisfying them. Therefore, it is the duty of an entrepreneur to keep a tab on the needs of people in its targeted market segments. He would have to keep in regular touch with them, read text about them in the print media, listen to their demands and complaints and above all, be sympathetic towards them while trying to sell his products and services to them. Successful marketers are those who can create the needs for those products and services, which the target customers might not require. It is a difficult task but proper understanding of the buyer behaviour and meticulous planning of marketing efforts could deliver coveted results for the marketer.

Henry Maslow had pointed out that these needs were satisfied by an individual in the order described above. However, many exceptions to this order have been found in the annals of history, which indicate that these needs may not be proponent in an individual in this order. It also gives such examples related to tourism administration as are related to the needs defined by Maslow.

At one time, only one need is proponent in the mind of an individual. A child cannot ask for food and at the same time, demand a bicycle. First of all, he may take the bicycle and have fun with his friends. After his return, he may bother his mother for food. You must keep this basic concept in mind. The most proponent need of the prospective customer must be satisfied first. After satisfying that need, the very next need in the order of importance is to be satisfied. If the order dictated by the customer or the prospective customer is disturbed, the marketing gimmick may fail and the marketer may end up wasting his precious time, money and other resources.

There is another important concept related to wants. All the needs may not be manifested in terms of wants. Someone (preferably, marketing or manufacturing firm) may have to convert a need into a want. If a need is converted into a want, then only that firm would be able to satisfy the need of that particular customer. If the firm becomes a pioneer in terms of converting a need into a want, it could become one of the most successful entrepreneurs the mankind may have ever seen! How, for example, the want for a cellular phone was generated around the world? In fact, there was a need for communicating while being on the move and the executive, housewife or any person could not have waited to stand in a queue and call through a public call office. The element of grace and "high- end" was attached later to the cellular communication mode. The primary objective was to save time while moving (a primary need).

The secondary objective was to talk to the person (associated in business or at home) as and when the need arose (the secondary need). These twin objectives were achieved through a cellular phone (the want). The want was created in the markets of Europe through media blitzkrieg and exclusive features of cellular phones (the chief among them being the ability to talk while on the move). The cellular mania took the European markets by storm during the early eighties as a result of the excruciating marketing efforts of Siemens, AirTel, Nokia, Samsung and Panasonic. This war of nerves still goes on in the emerging markets of Asia. Can we create the need for such products also as are not required by the human race? The marketer need not work hard to create the need for tobacco, alcohol and other vices. But if we answer the aforementioned question in the negative, then the marketer would state, "My uncle is in liquor business and he is the best person in the entire world !" We would contend that no business is bad.

However, while choosing a business stream, we would have to take into account our educational background, the reputation of our parents, financial resources available, suggestions of our friends and relatives and above all, our abilities (as well as limitations). You cannot jump into the liquor business simply because there is a great demand for liquor or because our uncle has been successful in this business. Further, we know that liquor consumption is bad for health. We would have to give a serious thought to acceptance of our products and services by the society in the light of legal, environmental and broad societal constraints in which, it thrives. Example: The need of a person is hunger. He can satisfy his need by consuming a burger. So, his want is a burger. The firm that manufactures burgers can deliver a message in the targeted markets (which would reach that hungry person) that burgers can satisfy the hunger of a hungry man. So, instead of consuming bread, *chapati,* lentils or vegetables, the hungry man can eat burgers (want) to satiate his hunger (need).

We would like to come back to the concept of wants. We want to satisfy the needs of the targeted markets through the products or services demanded by them (the wants). And just like new needs can be created, new wants can also be created among the targeted market niches. We can get an edge over our competitors by creating a different want for satisfying the same need of our customers. Example: We can sell cola drinks and beat the competition who might be selling orange drinks. The need remains the same-thirst. The wants (of buyers) would change-from orange drink (sold by the competitor) to cola drink (sold by us).

Types of Demands : Demand is a want for a specific product that is backed up by an ability and willingness to buy it. Example: If hunger is the need and burger is the want, then the demand of the person in question could be McDonald's Burger.

Demand can be of 4 types, as follows :—

Actual : It is that real demand that can be calculated by judging the past trends of the market. It is the demand for a product or service (in a given market niche) according to the current trends. There will be only minor changes in this demand, if we extrapolate the trends of the past into the future.

Latent : It is the demand that can be satisfied in future but is not known even to the targeted market niches.

New : It is the demand that can be created with respect of new products and services. These products and services have not arrived in the market as yet. But the demand for the same would have to be created first and then, these would have to be supplied to the targeted markets.

Negative : It is the demand for those products that the customer does not need. Rather, he shuns the use of such products. The demand for some of these products ought to be created in the interest of the welfare of a community or society. Examples: Family planning programmes, insurance policies.

***Satisfaction of Need* :** A product is something that can satisfy a need or want. All the products deliver services. A shaving blade is of no use unless it cleans the stubble of a man. A transport fleet is useless if it does not deliver the goods of a client in time.

Products are of many types and varieties. The buyers of these products try to buy those very products that can satisfy their actual needs. They may not be keen to buy those products that do not satisfy their needs or those that do not seem to be satisfying their needs. Products and services are available from the markets of the world. But only those products and services would be sold to the clients that meet their needs. The desperate seller of such goods and services may make efforts to create needs of products and services to garner profits' for his enterprise. In that event, needs are created. Such needs lead to wants. These wants, in turn, lead to demand. This is the most glaring feature of business operations going) around the globe.

You can satisfy the needs of the customers, which eventually become wants, through the products and services manufactured and sold by you. We would also include thoughts (or concepts) in this set. Religious affiliation with a temple or church is basically a thought. However, products and services are also important.

Products and services satisfy the needs of a person. Both of them deliver services—tangible and intangible. The marketer would be required to understand their needs and judge whether their wants are matching their needs or not (they might be wrong as well). After clearly understanding what the target markets want, the marketer should create such products or services as could satisfy these needs and wants. Products and services must be delivered at the right time, in the right quantity, with the right package and at the right place to the customer-to-be.

4

MARKETING CHANNELS

PRODUCERS OF PRODUCT

They are the airlines, hotels, airlines, cruise lines, coach operators, taxis, ferries, resorts, museums, forts, palaces, heritage hotels, zoos, wildlife parks, bird sanctuaries etc that are the attractions for tourists. Because of a fascination for these, the tourist undertakes tours. These producers give products and services of various kinds to the tourist. But most of these are services. Items placed in the shops of shopping malls (of a tourist spot) are products. Food items, liquor, wines and water and also products. Attraction, research, exploration, social reasons (like marriages and meetings with friends) could be the reasons to undertake tours. Producer of these products and services sign tie-up agreements with channels of distribution so that they could sell their (products and services). They cannot go to the targeted marketers every now and then. They call use high-end magazines and newspapers to build nice images in the minds of prospective customers. But they normally depend upon the wholesalers (tour operators) and retailers (travel agencies) to actually sell these products and services. Airlines (producers of transport services) also sell their tickets directly to customers.

Instance: Jagson Airlines. Most of the airlines have the accreditation of the *IATA.*; in fact, tourists do not go to such airlines as do not have such types of accreditation.

Wholesalers of Products

They buy various services of producers, or get reservations done for these services. They buy in bulk (allow prices) and that is why, they earn a lot (because they sell these services at much higher prices). They are normally called Tour Operators. They remain in touch with airlines, hotels, resort owners, discotheques, private spot owners and people involved in special sports (like parasailing, bungee jumping, kayaking, paragliding etc). They also buy tickets for State-operated tourist spots or sites. In this context, tickets for forts, museums, rope way transport systems, palaces and other ancient monuments can be considered. But if the government does not sell these tickets in advance, the executives of tour operators, buy these tickets for travel agents at such spots. Customers do not have to pay for these tickets because they have already paid for the same while buying their tour packages. Tour operators seldom deal with customers; they interact with travel agents most of the times. One tour operator can have many travel agents in its fold. These travel agents are not owned by the tour operator and their business dealings with the tour operator are based on commission percentages. In many countries, specialty chancellors buy the services of producers in bulk and sell them to other wholesalers, who operate at much lower levels.

RETAILERS OF PRODUCTS

They are the travel agents that buy services from wholesalers (tour operators). One travel agent may be associated with many tour operators simply because different tour operators may be catering to different tourism sectors. Travel agencies interact with customers on a day-to-day basis. They also send their executives to the homes and offices of clients or prospective clients. These executives undertake the real selling jobs, unlike the executives of tour operators who sell only to travel agencies. Services form a major part of any tourism package. Customers are free to buy products' when they are on tour. Some of the products (like breakfast, welcome drinks, dinner, complementary lunch etc.) are included in tour packages. Some travel agents are known for their excellent services. Thus, they grow because of their brand names. Some travel agencies also buy the services of producers in bulk. Thus, at times, they also act as tour operators (wholesalers). Not all travel agencies try to become tour operators because the risk involved in buying services (from producers).

The physical distribution channel in tourism is somewhat similar to the one in conventional marketing. However, actual goods and services are not provided to customers in their offices, homes, or at the retail stores (as is the case in conventional marketing). The tourist buys the services from travel agents that plan the entire programme for him. The bookings for airlines, hotels, resorts, fun parks, zoos, lakes, wildlife parks etc., are done in advance. The tourist also pays for these in advance. Then, on the stipulated day, he leaves his home (station of origin). He arrives at the destination station according to the terms mentioned in the tour itinerary. The agents of the travel agency or tour operator help him arrive at the hotel or spot where he is supposed to arrive. The tour itinerary is strictly followed (by the agents of the travel agency or tour operator). The producers of various goods and services provide these goods and services according to the itinerary. Such arrangements (bookings) are made even before the tourist leaves the station of origin. He can move from one destination station to another but according to the itinerary. He has no choice of changing the itinerary once he has finalised it (in most of the cases). At the end of the itinerary, the tourist is taken back to the station of origin according to the details mentioned in the itinerary.

Further, note that some tourists may not like to come back to the station of origin. Foreigners quite often plan their tours in this manner. They buy one-way tickets and move to the destination station. From the destination station, they can be on their own or associated with another travel agency. Such tour combinations are clearly planned and made known to all the staff members of the concerned travel agencies or tour operators. Finally, producers of tourism services are not liable to provide any other service that is beyond the gamut of their operations. Examples: A hotel would not take a tourist to a tourist spot within the city because it is not the duty of the hotel staff to do so. The travel agency must appoint a man (guide or coach driver) to take the tourist to that spot (according to the itinerary). Hotels are also not responsible for half-day sight seeing tours; such tours are the exclusive responsibilities of travel agencies that are running the entire show. Travel agencies also buy tickets for zoos, forts, lakes, palaces, historical monuments for their clients (tourists). If this is not possible, then the tourist is informed (at the station of origin) that he would be required to buy such tickets from his own pocket.

Emanation of Marketing Environment : The concept of marketing environment emanates from the broader concept of business environment.

MACRO-ENVIRONMENT

Marketing environment of a firm consists of the external factors and forces that affect the company's ability to develop and maintain successful transactions and relationships with its target markets. This definition was given by Phillip Kotler in his famous book *Marketing Management: Analysis, Implementation and Control*, 6th Ed, 1989, Prentice Hall. There are two parts of this environment, according to Kotler-internal environment and external environment.

Micro-environment **:** The microenvironment of the firm comprises the following.

The Firm: It is a part of the microenvironment. Its human resource, plant, machines, offices, retail outlets and equipment are a part of its microenvironment; so are its procedures, policies and strategies.

Suppliers: These are vendors who supply goods, services and professional advice to the firm in the context of its operations.

Marketing Intermediaries: These include middlemen, physical distribution channels and financial intermediaries.

Customers: These are the most important component of the microenvironment. The firm earns profits by selling its products and services to them. Consumer Behaviour has been discussed in detail in this section.

Competitors: There are 4 types of competitors-Desire Competitors (based on the desire to be satisfied), Generic competitors (depending upon the product the clients would like to consume), Form Competitors (depending upon the form or format of the product offered) and Brand competitors (depending upon the preference of clients for particular brands).

Public: A public is a group that has an actual or potential interest or impact on the ability of a firm to achieve its objectives. There are many types of public, namely, financial publics (like banks, investment houses and financial institutions), media public (like newspapers and TV channels), government publics (like government departments, commissions and ministries), citizen action publics (like NGOs, environmental action groups and minority associations), local publics (like neighbourhood associations), internal publics (like blue collar workers, white *collar* managers, the top brass and managers) of the firm and general public (people at large in a society or nation).

Behaviour of Consumer

Before we delve deeply into the realms of buying behavioural let us study consumer characteristics.

Characteristics of Consumer

The following characteristics are associated with consumers of all categories.

GEOGRAPHIC FEATURES

Geographic Situation and Terrain : Geographic data can often provide clues for an effective segmentation strategy. The geographical terrain of a market segment would decide the type of products or services to be sold in that area. Problems related to logistics would also have to be sorted out before the firm starts its marathon run in a market. Hills and mountains are a pretty tough terrain for all types of marketers. Snow--clad mountains and regions also need many products and services like liquor, woolens, shoes, trekking gear, radio paging systems, medicines, high-calorie foods etc. Deserts need different kind of treatment; so do marshes, plains of the rivers and plateaus of the world.

The marketer has to collect the geographical data of the targeted region first. Then, he must find out how this data affects the buying habits and motives of the targeted (or prospective) clients living in that very region. And he must remember that Mother Nature can be very harsh at some places. Mountains and an uneven terrain may not be the cup of tea of many a tourist.

Size of Country : This is also a vital factor in determining the associated with buyers.

Size of City : Large city sizes would force consumers to buy more items of necessity. Luxury needs would also increase in terms of quantity and quality.

Determination of Products by Climate and Weather : It is obvious that weather and climate would also determine the types of products that would be demanded by customers. Rainfall, snowfall, heat etc., would determine he types of products that the customers may ask for.

Density of Population

A higher population density would warrant the consumption of more products of a particular category. Climate would also play an important part in this context.

Natural Calamities

Natural calamities like deluge, draught, thunderstorm, typhoon, excessive snowfall etc., would lead to the demand of such products as would help people survive during the tenures of those calamities.

Demographic Features

A very basic but useful demographic feature of man is age.

Classification of Customers by Age

Stage in Life Demand	*Age Group*	*Tourism*
Infancy	0-5 years	Nil
Childhood	8-12 years	Local
Adolescence	13-17 years	Local; regional
Adulthood	18-40 years	regional; national; international
Middle Age	41-50 years	National; international
Old Age	51-70 years	National; international
Veteran	71-100 years	Nil
Vintage	>100 years	Nil

The senior citizen market is growing around the world and a host of their needs and wants are not being fulfilled by existing products and services. These grey markets need special attention, products, services. In the West, these people are the privileged ones. But they are not looked after in countries like India where their population is on the rise. Another important market niche is that of young adults. They are the most eligible candidates for undertaking activities related to tourism. They are not keen to undertake religious tours. Nowadays, they are more keen to undertake foreign tours, albeit only for a few days. Little children and infants are the candidates for diapers, toys, chocolates and all things entertaining and glossy. But their parents take decisions at many occasions. ***Instance :*** They may refuse to buy chocolates and potato chips for their 7-year-old daughter who needs it badly while the family is on a tour. So, the marketer may have to target his advertising campaigns and pricing strategies towards the parents (decision makers) and not children (ultimate consumers). That is because the former may be taking most of the purchase decisions on behalf of the latter.

Veterans are keen to undertake religious tours. They may also show interest in archeological sites, forts, palaces, museums and ancient excavation sites. The youth may not show keen interest in the rich historical relics of the tourist spot being visited by them.

Income : Another useful demographic criterion is income. The table below gives the latest data on income classes of the world.

It is obvious that people in the higher income brackets would be tempted to undertake tours of foreign countries. People of lower income brackets would like to travel within the regions of their residence. They may take extra pains' to undertake religious tours to far off places, however. ***Instance:*** A resident of Jammu may take his parents to Puri and let them visit jagannath temple. His parents may have requested their son to help them complete the journey of *char dhamas* (Puri, Dwarka, Badrinath and Rameshwaram). People of middle income groups use trains to travel while rich people prefer aircraft and their own four-wheelers. Local taxis and auto-rickshaws are used by all the categories' of people because they are not well versed with the environs of the place visited. They do not mind Paying for this luxury because:

(a) they know that they are not going to visit that spot time and again and thus, spending on taxis and auto-rickshaws is justified at least at the tourist spot/city; and

(b) they are more keen to ensure the comfort of the family members who may be travelling along with them.

Instance: A tourist family from Gujarat may visit Goa and see the important churches, beaches and temples. It may use the services of a taxi/van so that it could complete the tour in time.

Foreign tourists prefer coaches and taxis to move about in a city. They can afford the high costs of travel; moreover, they are dependent upon tour operators and travel agencies in respect of local sightseeing tours and excursions to wildlife sanctuaries.

Gender : There are two types of customer, if gender is the sole criterion of segregation-male and female. Ladies and girls may have special requirements like privacy, pleasant behaviour, respect, special clothes, medicines, escort, security in the hotel, company of kith and kin etc. Men and boys, on the other hand, are independent, ego-stricken, go-getters, explorers, willing and able to take risks; ready to take risks and above all, rough and tough. But in the new millennium, the differentiating line between men and women has been erased to a great extent. **Instance:** Women, like men, like bungee jumping. We have found many men avoiding this sport but women have willing volunteered to undertake the fall! SD, the modern-day woman must not be taken lightly, especially when she is on a tour.

Occupation : The type of occupation creates a distinct psyche in the mind of the customer. His decisions are moulded according to, the job he is doing. Example: An executive would buy the finest of perfumes but a labourer may never show interest in them.

Educated People : Highly educated people are demanding and quality conscious. Illiterate people may not give consideration to quality and hence, are eligible to be given cheap low-quality products and services.

People of Different Religion : The religion of a person bars him from consuming some products and forces him to follow a unique life-style. The buyer would act according to his religious influences in the Third World countries, especially India.

People of Different Race : People of different races have different orientations toward products and services. Their attitudes may have been gelled by their religious thoughts as well.

Life Cycle of Family : The stage in the Family life cycle would persuade the customer to buy different products and services.

Size of Family : The number of persons living in a family (on a permanent basis) would affect the buying patterns of the family as a whole.

People of Different Nations : People of different nations would prefer different types of products and services.

Psychographic Nature

There are 5 major characteristics in this category, as follows.

Cultural Factors

Factors deeply associated with culture are vital when multinational firms attempt to develop a segmentation strategy with the world as large market. Differences among cultures can affect important processes such as product acceptance and post-purchase behaviour. Example: Tourists cannot eat pork in a Muslim country like Malaysia, the UAE, Kuwait and Saudi Arabia. In Europe, it is customary to attend a burial in black clothes (which signify death and mourning) and not white ones (which signify peace and prosperity).

Style of Living : A person's interests, opinions and activities combine to represent his or her life-style.

Knowledge of life-styles of the targeted customers can provide vital data about a person or group of persons. It can indicate whether the person is keen to take part in outdoor sports, shopping, theatre or parasailing. It can also include information concerning attitudes and personality traits of the person being studied. Life-style affects the buying behavior of the person in the sense that the person in question wants to have at least the same level of comfort as he had been enjoying in the past. He may long for higher levels of comfort and luxury. But he would certainly not like to do away with his existing set of gadgets, luxury goods, clothes and habits. This is a good clue for all the tourism marketers. A direct outcome of this analysis is-give your customer what he already has (or prefers) but do not forget to show him what he doesn't have (or may prefer).

Factors of Whims and Fancies

Here we are! We know that these are the most important indicators of buyers' motives. Some women hate red socks but some others keep on wearing them even in the bed! Man is a strange creature. His behaviour is unpredictable at many moments. If the marketer can somehow understand how he would behave at particular occasions, he can give the products and services of the finest quality to him. And in this process, he would satisfy the most hidden desires of man, thus earning for himself fortunes beyond imagination. But judging the whims of humans is very difficult process. Many firms have failed in the past in this task.

This brings us to a vital question-how can hotel staff learn about the whims and fancies of a guest who has just checked in ? In such cases, when it is not possible to judge the preferences of the guest or customer, it is imperative to get an idea from that customer as soon as he arrives at the scene. The hotel staff can talk to the customer when he checks in. His preferences for vegetarian and non-

-vegetarian food can be noted. His tour programme can also be jotted down so that the staff is aware when he would check out of the hotel. If the guest prefers blue colour, then, the staff can provide him a bed with a blue bedspread. This has to be done despite the fact that all the hotels use white linen in their rooms. If the guest is given sops like these, he feels important as his whims are satiated. And he is ready to pay for these extras.

Diverse Personality

Different types of personality would lead to different types of behaviours. The person could be an autocrat, gregarious, ambition or compulsive. Accordingly, his motivations for purchasing goods and/or services would defined.

Different Social Classes

People belonging to the lower-lower class would demand different products than those belonging to the upper-upper class. Class conflict would also play a major role while the customer buys products or services. ***Instance:*** A tourists belonging to the upper crust would travel by luxury class in an aircraft but a person of the middle income class would prefer the economy class.

Characteristics of Behavioural Consumer : This category of consumer characteristics is more closely associated with the purchasing process itself. The following characteristics are noteworthy.

Rate of Usage

A powerful segmentation variable is the usage rate of product or service. The marketer must find out who are the heavy users of his products or services and who are the light users of the same. The most interesting of all the targeted customers are the non-users. The challenge is to get them to try the product and ultimately, make them heavy users. Table below Gives the profile of all the types of users according to the degree of usage of a product or service.

The marketing manager must address at least two problems in this context :-

(A) Development of such programs as attract members of targeted groups, or niches to try the product for the first time.

(B) Develop products or services that this group would like to buy regularly.

(C) Motivate non-users to trap in his marketing net.

(D) Try to pluck customers from the trees of customers in a sophisticated decent manner so that the latter do not cry 'foul.'

(E) Convert light users into medium users and medium users into heavy users.

Status of Loyalty

There are 4 categories in the parlance of loyalty status- None, Medium, Strong, Absolute. This classification was done by Phillip Kotler. The loyalty status has many iminuations, which can be explained in the context of an example from the tourism industry. Example: When a brand such as Cox & Kings is competing in a well-defined class such as package tours, it is useful to consider brand loyalty as a basis for segmentation. The customers of Cox & Kings can be divided into two distinct classes-those who are loyal buyers of the brand and those who are not. The disloyal buyer tends to buy several brands, selecting, for example, the least expensive or the most convenient brand at the moment of purchase. Similarly, non-users of Cox & Kings can also be divided into two classes-those, who are loyal only to particular brands and those, who buy several other brands at random. The marketer has to increase brand loyalty to his own brand by persuading brand loyalists of other brands. He has also to target the marketing campaigns to those fickle-minded customers who do not have a well-defined pattern of purchase. We have observed that tourists go to a different travel agency for purchasing air tickets. They want to find out whether rates given by the previous travel agent were correct or not. Once they find a particular travel agency that gives them the best prices, they stick to it (an example of absolute loyalty). The same is true for holiday packages as well. Once the customer is convinced about the rates, efficient planning, courtesy and picture-perfect execution of a travel agency, he goes to it for undertaking another tom. Over a period of years, brand loyalists identify themselves with these travel agencies or hotels. They stay only at those hotels with which, their experiences in the past had been pretty good. Rarely, if ever, they change their preferences, they come back to the original set of hotels, travel agents etc. The marketer has to build brand loyalty among its corporate clientele by sending them mailers and letters on a regular basis. He can tell them about special discounts that he can offer to them. He can also give them extra sops like free accommodation for children, cold drinks, liquor, welcome breakfast, gifts in lieu of the brand loyalty that he gets from such customers. Many corporate clients are being served by reputed travel agencies of India in this manner.

Tourism products are perishable in nature. Customers are aware of this fact. They do not want to take risk while they select tour packages for themselves and their families. They want to get the best out of the package tour selected by them. That is because they cannot retrace their steps back to square one, once they have committed to undertake such tours. The task of the marketer is to convince the customer that the package being bought by him would give him the full value of money. It is, however, not an easy task. Customers withdraw their bookings many times, even if they have to forego some booking amount that is already with the travel agent. In our view, if the customer is an old one, he should be given the booking amount even if he does not undertake the tour due to one reason or the other. This would help the marketer get another order from him in the future. The buyer wants reliability of the marketer (travel agency or hotel) because he knows that the product is perishable. Finally, if the advance amount cannot be returned to him, as is true in the cases of foreign tours, the marketer should give the customer some additional facilities so that the customer does not feel that he has been fleeced due to a wrong decision taken by him. He can be convinced that he would do well to undertake the tour that he has planned to cancel and that he would be given additional discount in the next tour. The travel agent can help the customer book the air ticket and hold seat for him for 14 days without paying a penny. But if the customer has not been able to change the departure schedule even after this limit, the travel agent must convince him that it is better to fly on the same ticket, lest he should lose money by way of cancellation charges.

Social Considerations

Social considerations are important when we discuss tourism as an activity for intermingling of various types of people. Every tourist in a group belongs to a different social set-up. These different social set-ups are able to create sets of beliefs in the minds of individuals. They cannot do away with these beliefs simply because they are visiting a foreign country. Even within a country like India, we can witness different societal forces acting at all the times on individuals.

Instance: A south Indian would love to wear a *dhoti* even if he has checked into a hotel of Shimla. For him, wearing a *dhoti* is a status symbol. His social beliefs have made him think that way. But the locals may not like his habit.

Instance: Some south Indians take food while sitting on the floor, without spoons and after some initial rituals like *pula*. But in a hotel of north India, they may seem to be out of place; it is not their native state, after all.

Instance: North Indians may not consume food or snacks prepared by *Dallies*.

The tourism marketer has to understand these beliefs of the targeted markets. Then, he must understand how these beliefs can be consolidated when the guest is making use of his services or consuming his products. He must address these problems and issues that are registered by his customer from time to time. Eventually, he would arrive at a set of beliefs or habits that a particular social group follows. This would be done over a period of time, after meeting lot many customers of a particular societal niche. Thus, the marketer would evolve a set of strategies to cater to the precise needs of that group. Similarly, he would define strategies for other groups that are his frequent or regular customers. Time would teach him these vital lessons.

Stage for Being Ready

The important parameters in this category ate-unaware, Aware, Informed, Interested, Desirous and Intending to Buy.

Consumer's Attitude's towards Product : : The important parameters in this category are—Enthusiastic, Positive, Indifferent, Negative and Hostile.

Status of Users

The important parameters in this category are-Non-user, Ex-user, Potential User, First-time User and Regular User.

Special Occasions

The important parameters in this category are-Special Occasions and Regular Occasions.

Advantages Sought

The important parameters in this category are-Quality, Image building of Self, Service, Economy, Eco-friendly Disposition and Convenience.

Legal Factors in Travel

These are the factors that govern the travel, stay, excursion, movements, purchases and other activities of a tourist in a foreign land. Even within a country, the rules of various state can differ from those of another state. The United States has *50* different Stales and each one of those has a different set of rules, though these are a part of the Big Apple. Rules related to octroi, entry and exit of foreigners, customs duties, airport taxes, rules for stay in a hotel, check out timings, rules for declaration of excess baggage, forms to be filled to declare special goods (while arriving at a new station or airport), halt at transit airports, entry into strategic places cantonments and rules for extradition of wily tourists or foreigners are different for different countries.

The marketer has to understand and imbibe the basic spirit of each and every rule that is associated with tourism. Then, he must communicate these rules to the targeted clients during the course of the marketing campaign. He may also have to communicate the same when the customer is being served by him.

That is because many tourists are not aware of the laws of the land and may commit mistakes during their tours. Safe hassle-free passage of the customer is the responsibility of the marketer; so, he must have a legal advisor/counsel to give him legal support. This would ensure that the customer does not face any problem during the itinerary. Legal factors are always in the back of the mind of every tourist. These control his actions and behaviour whenever he travels to a foreign land.

5

SALE NETWORK

Travel agency sector is the distributor element in the travel and tourism marketing system. It can be considered to be a link between the producers of various travel services like tour operators, airline companies, transport operators and hoteliers on the one hand and their customers on the other. In other words, travel agents bring buyers and sellers together with a view to creating markets in places where these did not exist or to make existing markets more user friendly and efficient in order to expand the overall size of the travel market.

Today, the travel agent has become an important, integral, part of the travel and tourism industry world wide. Majority of people are using the services of travel agents for organising their travel both international as well as domestic. It is estimated that worldwide almost 70% of all international travel and 45% of all domestic travel are arranged by the travel agents. The figure however, may vary from country to country. The important role of the travel agent in the modern world is summarised in the principles of professional conduct and ethics of the American Society of Travel Agents. The role of travel agents in summarised as follows :

"We live in a world in which travel has become increasingly important and complex in its variety of modes and choices. Travellers are faced with a myriad alternatives as to transportation, accommodation and other travel services. They must depend on travel agencies and others in the industry to guide them honestly and competently."

Product Selling

The main function of a travel agency is the product sale. Product sale is very complex subject specially when the product happens to be a tourist product. Because of the special nature of the tourist product and the multiplicity of manufacturers of the product, selling assumes greater importance. In addition, the distribution channels through which the tourist product finds its way to the consumers are multiple and varied. The tourist product, consists mainly of attractions, transport and accommodation. The producers of elements of the above products include air, sea, road transport companies and carriers, hotels and other forms of accommodation units, and the organisations which are responsible for putting together attractions both natural and man-made.

In most of the countries product sale is conducted through a distribution system controlled mostly by a network of retail travel agents, tour operators and wholesalers. The individual elements of a tourist product like international air tickets, domestic air or train tickets are also mostly sold through agents or representatives of airlines and railway companies, and purchased directly by consumers. The consumers have, therefore, a choice between direct booking and using the services of an agent. In addition, there are alternative channels available to the consumers through which they may buy their tourism products. These channels include clubs and societies, mail order, travel shops in supermarkets and departmental stores, tourist fairs and exhibitions and, more recently, electronic booking methods like computers.

Past Perspective

Any discussion on sale and organisation of travel must begin with the pioneer named Thomas Cook. The history of the business of the present Thomas Cook Group Limited can be traced back to over 150 years to its founder Thomas Cook, who not only was the first organised Travel Agent in the world, but who, it could be said, invented the travel business. A book salesman, a baptist preacher of Derbyshire was on his way to a temperance meeting in Leicester when he was inspired with "the idea of engaging a special train to carry the friends of temperance from Leicester to Loughborough in England and back to attend a quarterly delegate meeting." He thought that it was a sounder proposition to persuade a railway company, then in its infancy, to carry a train load of passengers at a very cheap fare than to run the train at 'standard' fares, but possibly only a quarter full. The man was Thomas Cook and his idea was put into operation with characteristic speed and efficiency. A few weeks later 570 travellers made the journey by the Midland Counties Railway at a specially reduced fare. This venture was soon followed by excursions to various other places, and in 1843, 3,000 school children were taken on a trip from Leicester to Derby in England.

Thomas Cook's real beginning as 'mass excursionist' was, however, the Liverpool-Caernaryon trip of 1845. The tourists travelled by rail to Liverpool, from where they took a steamer to Caernaryon. The advertisements for the trip caused a sensation and the response was so overwhelming that a second trip had to be arranged. Cook thought of every detail. He made a preliminary survey of accommodation and facilities and produced a handbook of the trip to Liverpool. The excursionist invasion of Scotland soon followed in 1846 and 1847. From 1848 to 1863 Cook conducted circular tours of Scotland, with 5,000 tourists a season. With the citadels of the landed aristocracy falling before him, he saw more enticing prospects opening before him: "I had become so thoroughly imbued with the tourist spirit that I began to contemplate Foreign Trips, including the continent of Europe, the United States and the Eastern land of the Bible."

Circular Route

By the mid-nineteenth century 'Holidays away from home' had become customary for a larger social group than ever before. Cook's initiative and organising genius provided the final impetus. In the winter of 1850-51, Cook was already negotiating for a tour of America, but his attention was diverted when he was offered the opportunity of conducting excursion trains to the Great Exhibition of 1851. Altogether, Cook conducted 1,65,000 people to and from the Crystal Palace. In 1856, Cook succeeded in organising his First grand circular tour of the continent. The tour was so successful that it had to be repeated six weeks later.

Thomas Cook's conquest of Europe began in 1862 when he made arrangements with Brighton and South Coast Railway for passenger traffic to the continent. Cook's Paris excursions are the first true 'package tours'; all the details of transport and accommodation were pre-arranged. In 1863 Cook visited Switzerland where his ideas were greeted with enthusiasm by hoteliers and railway proprietors. His next stop was Italy. Cook first made a personal survey of Turin, Milan, Florence and Genoa, to familiarise himself with their touristic attractions and facilities. In 1864 the first guided tour of Italy left England with applications far in excess of the available tickets. The 1860s also saw the introduction of Cook's 'railway and hotel coupons'. Cook personally examined the system by travelling through Italy to Vienna, down the Danube into Hungary and from there into Switzerland. By the 1890s, 1,200 hotels throughout the world accepted his coupons. Starting in 1868 Cook arranged regular circular tours of Switzerland and Northern Italy.

The first official London Office of Thomas Cook and Sons was established in 1865. John Mason Cook now joined his father as a permanent partner and took charge of the London office. From that year on, the history of Thomas Cook and Sons was one of continuous expansion. In the year 1880 John Mason Cook left for India and established offices in Bombay and Calcutta and formed the 'Eastern Princes' Department. In 1887 this department arranged the visits of Indian princes to Queen Victoria's Jubilee Celebrations.

By taking advantage of nineteenth century advances in transport technology, Thomas Cook and Sons had effected a revolution in tourism by the end of the century. No longer the preserve of the rich and the aristocrats, tourism was now an industry. Armed with Cook's hotel and rail coupons, the tourist could demand uniform prices and standards of service and accommodation. This new standardisation had distinct advantages. It meant comfort and convenience and less need for decision making on the part of the individual tourist. The tourist was less likely to experience discomfort or embarrassment.

The management of the Company passed on to John Mason Cook's three sons in the year 1898. At the time of John Mason Cook's death, the business included three main aspects of travel -selling tours, banking and shipping. Soon after the Second World War, the British government acquired the principal interest in the Company. In the year

1972, the British Government sold the company to Midland Bank Consortium.

Today, Thomas Cook Group is the parent company of a worldwide group of companies which are partially or wholly owned. The company also has a close trading relationship with Companie International des Wagon-Lits et Tourism, and the combined worldwide network of these companies, together with their authorised agents. The company also introduced traveller's cheques which were originally called 'circular notes'. Members of the Thomas Cook Group of companies now issue cheques as principals in different currencies and are associated with partner banks in various countries. It is also a large trader in the buying and selling of foreign currency bank notes. Thomas Cook Group Limited today provides a wide range of services to its customers in over 150 countries worldwide through their network of over 1,200 outlets. The company is considered to be one of the largest travel companies selling a wide range of travel services.

Much has changed since the year 1841, when Thomas Cook chartered a train to carry 570 travellers at a specially reduced fare from Leicester to Loughborough in England. Cook, who bought the railway tickets in bulk and resold them to members of his group, can be credited with being the first bona fide travel agent to work as a full-time professional. However, neither Thomas Cook & Sons, nor American Express Company or Cox and Kings were then a retail agent as the modern complex distribution chain had not yet evolved in any trade including travel.

Product Market

The scope and the role of the travel agency was limited in the beginning since mass tourism as we know it today had not yet begun. It was, however, the introduction of the air travel which gave a boost to the travel agency business. The introduction of an economy class by various airline companies crossing the North Atlantic heralded the era of travel agency and was responsible for their growth. The introduction of an 'economy class' in effect was nothing more than a projection of Thomas Cook's original idea of adjusting prices to encourage full capacity use of every means of transport.

Rapid development of transport system, especially the jet travel, improved living standards combined with reduction in working hours is the root cause of today's upward surge in travel. Side by side with the rapid improvements in industry and technology, practically all aspects of life have become more and more complex particularly during the past half a century. This is certainly the case in the travel industry in which, only a century ago, the job consisted almost entirely of arranging a simple reservation for the travellers in some means of transport. Today the functions and duties of a person at the travel agency counter are vastly different and more varied. He is now called upon to perform a variety of duties rather than just issue tickets and reserve seats in a train, aeroplane or accommodation in the hotel. Travel today is no longer the privilege of the few, but is sought by millions. No longer does the travel agency exist for the sole purpose of selling tickets from one point to another. The travel industry developed along certain well-defined lines as the worldwide demand on its services increased. The urge to travel became very intense over the years resulting in wide-spread growth of travel agencies in the world. Most of the travellers wished to have their travel arrangements made in advance and to be relieved of the difficulties of coping with various pre-travel arrangements of which they had only a very limited knowledge.

Recent Trends

Over the years the range and activities of a retail travel agent have increased manifold. In the modern context, the role of a travel agent is rather different to that of most of other retailers selling merchandise. The travel agent does not purchase travel with a view to reselling the same to its customers. It is only when a customer has finally decided on the purchase of travel that the agent approaches the principal on behalf of his customer. The retail travel agent, unlike most other retailers, does not carry an inventory or stock of travel products in his premises.

The main role of retail travel agents is to provide to their customers a convenient location for the "purchase" of various elements of travel like transport, accommodation and several other ancillary services associated with holiday and travel. The travel agents act as booking agents for holidays and travel and disseminate information and give advice on such services. This role can be summed up as follows:

(i) to give advice to the potential tourist on the merits of alternative destinations, and

(ii) to make necessary arrangements for a chosen holiday which may involve booking of accommodation, transport or other relevant services associated with his travel.

A travel agent, in order to give an advice to his potential customers on the merits of a destination, must possess knowledge, expertise and up-to-date information about that destination. Besides, a travel agent has close contacts with providers of services, i.e., their principals from whom they purchase services for their customers. In other words, a retail travel agent is an intermediary providing a direct link between the consumer and the suppliers of tourist services, i.e.., airlines, transport companies, hotels, auto rental companies, etc. The retail agent is the one who acts on behalf of the principal, i.e., the original provider of tourist service such as an airline company, hotel company, shipping company, insurance company, railways or a tour operator. An agent sells the principal's services and is rewarded by a commission.

Functions and Procedure

The scope and range of travel agency operations would depend on the size of an agency. If the company is large in size, the range of activities will be more comprehensive. In this case the agency will have specialised departments, each having to perform different functions. To deal with the subject of a travel agency, the best method of approach is, perhaps, to consider its functions. These may be broadly classified as follows:

Providing Information

One of the primary functions of a retail travel agent from the point of view of the tourist or the general public is to provide necessary information about travel. This information is provided at a convenient location where the intending tourist may ask certain questions and seek clarifications about his proposed travel. This is a very specialised job and the person behind the counter should be a specialist having excellent knowledge of various travel alternative plans. He should be in a position to give up-to-date and accurate information regarding various services and general information about travel, etc. The presentation to the potential customer must be forceful, and exciting variations must continually be devised to help sell tours. A good travel agent is something of a personal counsellor who knows all the details about the travel and also the needs and interests of the intending traveller. Communication plays a key role in dissemination of any type of information.

This is equally true in the case of dissemination of travel information. The person behind the travel counter should be able to communicate with the customer in his language. The knowledge of foreign languages is an essential prerequisite for personnel working in a travel agency.

Journey Records

Tourist itinerary is a composition of a series of operations that are a result of the study of the market. A tourist journey is characterised by an itinerary using various means of transport to link one locality with another. Preparation of different types of itineraries is another important function of a travel agency. A travel agent gives advice to intending travellers on the type of programmes which they may choose for their holiday or business travel. The study and the realisation of the itineraries call for perfect organisation (technical and administrative) as also knowledge of the desires of the public for a holiday and the propensity to receive tourists by the receiving localities.

Liaison with Providers of Services : Before any form of travel can be sold over the counter to a customer, contracts have to be entered into with the providers of various services. These include transportation companies, hotel proprietors, the providers of surface transport like motor cars or coaches for transfer to and from hotels and for sightseeing, etc., and also for general servicing requirements. The work carried out under these headings is usually that of the owners or senior employees of agencies concerned. In the case of a large agency with worldwide branches, the liaison work involves a great deal of coordination with the principals.

Frame Work

Once the contracts and arrangements have been entered into, there comes the task of planning and costing tours, both for inclusive programmes and to meet individual requirements. This job is intensely interesting and at the same time challenging. It calls for a great deal of initiative and drive, for travel to those places which are to be included in the itineraries. Paradoxically many of those who do this type of work visit comparatively few of the places included in the itineraries they prepare. This is essentially a job for a meticulous person and calls for considerable training and ability. Many agencies, with the cooperation of airlines and other transportation companies, take the opportunity of arranging educational tours for such staff to destinations with which they deal.

Many large agencies have experts who are authorities on particular countries and, in addition to a general programme, many will issue separate programmes dealing with specific territories. Separate programmes, dealing with holiday offers based on specific forms of transportation, e.g., air, rail, road or sea, may also be prepared. Programmes also have to be prepared to cover different seasons of the year.

Publicity is an important part of the programme. Having spent considerable time and money on preparing all that goes into the issue of a programme, publicity must feature considerably in the activities of a travel agency and more so if the agency happens to be a large one. The majority of large travel agencies have their own publicity departments under the management of an expert in the publicity field.

Ticketing : Selling tickets to clients using different modes of transport like air, rail and sea is yet another important function of a travel agency. This calls for a thorough knowledge of schedules of various modes of transport. Air carriers, railways and steamship companies have hundreds of schedules and the person behind the counter should be conversant with all these. Ticketing is, however, not an easy job as the range and diversity of international airfares is very complex and varied. There are several different types of fare combinations on the North Atlantic route alone. Changes in international as also in the local air schedules and additions of new flights from time to time makes the job of the travel agent one of constant challenge. An up-to-date knowledge about various schedules of air companies, steamship companies and railways is very essential.

Computerised reservation system has in recent years rather revolutionised the reservation system, both for air and rail seats, and also a room in a hotel. Many large travel agencies are using this system. This system comprises a computer network that can be used by the travel agent to reserve an air or rail accommodation as also accommodation in a hotel. Through a wide network, confirmation of reservations are available in a matter of seconds.

Settlement of Accounts : Linked with the function of ticketing and reservation of accommodation in a hotel is the settlement of accounts of the clients. Accountancy plays an important part and is one of the major duties to be performed by the travel agency. Dealing with the settlement of accounts in all parts of the world calls for a thorough knowledge of foreign currencies, their cross-values and, above all, the intricacies of exchange control regulations, which vary from country to country.

Provision of Foreign Currencies : Provision of foreign currencies to intending travellers is another specialised activity of a travel agency. Some of the larger travel agencies deal exclusively in the provision of foreign currencies, travellers' cheques, etc. This is an important facility to intending travellers as it saves them a lot of time and energy in avoiding visits to regular banking channels.

Insurance : Insurance, both for personal accident risks and of baggage, is yet another important activity of the travel agency. Some of the larger travel agents maintain sizeable shipping and forwarding departments, aimed at assisting the traveller, to transport personal effects and baggage to any part of the world, with a minimum of inconvenience.

The multifarious activities mentioned in the above paragraphs show that the travel agency's range of services in modern times has expanded a great deal. The field of expertise is quite large and is constantly growing with the fast changing travel needs of the people. The job description of a modern travel agency can be summed up as follows:

(i) Preparation of individual pre-planned itineraries, personally escorted tours and group tours and sale of pre- paid package tours.

(ii) Making arrangements for hotels, motels, resort accommodation, meals, car rentals, sightseeing, transfer of passengers and luggage between terminals and hotels, and special features such as music festivals and theatre tickets.

(iii) Handling of and giving advice on the many details involved in modern day travel, e.g., travel and baggage insurance, language study material, travellers' cheques, foreign currency exchange, documentary requirements (visas and passport) and health requirements (immunisation and inoculations).

(iv) Possession of professional knowledge and experience, as for instance, schedules of air and train connections, rates of hotels, their quality, whether rooms have baths, etc. All of this is information on which the traveller, but for the travel agent, will spend days or weeks of endless phone calls, letters and personal visits.

(v) Arrangement of reservations for special interest activities such as conventions, conferences, and business meetings and sports events, etc.

Organisation of Travelling

There are various activities which a travel agency has to perform in order that an intending traveller undertakes his proposed journey and enjoys a holiday of his choice. There are various steps involved from the time a traveller visits a travel agent to buy a ticket until he returns home after visiting a place of his choice.

Organised travel by a travel agency can be of two types, i.e. (i) single client, and (ii) group client. In order to effect the journey, the following main elements (in both types of travel) need to be considered:

(a) Study of the journey,

(b) Estimate of expenditure,

(c) Execution of the journey, and

(d) Presentation of accounts.

Individual or Ordinary Trips : The following steps are involved in organising individual or ordinary trips:

(i) The client turns to the travel agent to organise for him a particular journey (cultural, natural, business, religious, etc.).

(ii) The agency from this angle will examine as to what will be involved, e.g., scope of journey, when the journey is to take place, various services needed and the accessories required.

(iii) Based on the above evaluation and other elements in his possession, the travel agent will suggest an itinerary and will then communicate to the client the estimated maximum cost for the client's approval.

(iv) The travel agent will then compile the definite estimates, a total of a series of various costs added up, e.g., transport, accommodation, the services such as those of guides, operative costs such as (postage, telex, telefax, E-Mail, telephones, etc.).

(v) The travel agent then will present a document of the amount of money to be paid in duplicate to the customer. The client returns one of the debit copies signed on acceptance accompanied with a deposit (in anticipation). The deposit normally is about 25 per cent of the total cost.

(vi) Once the client's approval has been obtained, the travel agent's operation department then executes the journey.

(vii) The 'operation' department's task now is to book for the established dates the transport and various other services. After the booking confirmation has been received, the travel agent issues the vouchers.

(viii) The travel agent prepares the 'tourist itinerary' which will accompany the client through the entire journey. It will indicate the tickets to be used, the hotels and other services booked and will include vouchers, etc. Normally the itinerary is made in triplicate: one for the client, another for the agency and the third for the hotelier or those who will provide the required services paid by means of vouchers.

(ix) The last formality is the delivery to the client of the vouchers, confirmed tickets, the technical itinerary.

(x) When the group is particularly large, e.g., for sports, etc., the travel agent needs to take extra care by way of informing public authorities for purposes of security, etc.

Travel agents in a highly developed market cover all the above activities and range of services which depends upon the extent of the economic development of that country. The travel patterns of the population in advanced countries are different as compared to those in developing countries. The services of travel agents are increasingly utilised in developed countries. In some of the advanced countries like the USA, Canada, Germany and Japan a very large percentage of tourists are utilising the services of travel agents.

Tour Operators Role

The dramatic growth of tourist traffic to the Mediterranean countries of Europe is a principal feature of the history of mass tourism in the last forty years. A major contributing factor in this growth of air travel holiday tourism has been the development of 'inclusive tour', a method of packaging a holiday. The idea of buying a package of travel, accommodation and perhaps some ancillary services such as entertainment etc., became established in Western Europe in the 1960s. Essentially an 'inclusive tour' is a package of transport and accommodation and perhaps some other service which is sold as a single holiday for an all inclusive price. This inclusive price is usually significantly lower than could be obtained by conventional methods of booking transport and accommodation separately from individual hotel and transport tariffs. The principal feature of the inclusive tour is that the tourist may buy, for a single price, a holiday which is much cheaper than would be possible for the holiday maker if he bought the components of his holiday separately and directly from individual hotels and from transport companies or from a retail travel agent.

The chief functionary or the principal in this system is the tour operator. It is the tour operator who buys aircraft seats and hotel beds and certain other facilities such as surface transport or entertainment and makes up the package. Historically, the tour operator has mostly emerged from retail travel agency. However, today a clear distinction must be made between tour operator and a travel agent. The latter, the retail travel agent, undertakes to sell the travel services of his principal, who will be airline companies and other transport undertakings, hotel groups, shipping lines and the providers of such ancillary services as traveller's cheques, etc. Unlike the travel agent who is the retailer of the tourism product, the tour operator is a manufacturer of a tourism product. He plans, organises and sells tours. The tour operator makes all the necessary arrangements - transport, accommodation, sight-seeing, insurance, entertainment and other matters and sells this package for an all-inclusive price. A package tour is designed to fit a particular group of travellers. These may be special interest tours, i.e., mountain tours and can be escorted. Escorted tour normally includes transportation, meals, sightseeing, accommodation, guide services, etc. It is the escort or the group leader who is responsible for maintaining the schedule of the tour and for looking after all the arrangements.

Group Inclusive Tour (GIT) : This is the most popular form of tour in this category where people travel in groups of 15 or more persons. These tours are available for any destination. The terms and conditions for group inclusive tours are laid down by IATA. The escort for such groups normally travels free as the airline provides him with free passage and accommodation. "Foreign Inclusive Tours' (FIT) on the other hand are unescorted package tours. These tours are comparatively more flexible. The traveller can buy a predetermined package with arrangements for sightseeing, hotels and certain meals, where necessary. He does not tour with a group. He can make his own arrangements and programmes according to his liking. The inclusive tour is one of the several devices which enable tourists to enjoy the lower prices.

How does the tour operator manage to sell the package to the traveller at such a low price? The low price of the package holiday or inclusive tour is made possible by reason of the lower unit costs obtainable both for the air travel and for the hotel accommodation. The tour operator enters into long-term contracts for aircraft seats and similar contracts with hotels for booking rooms. By mass-producing holidays in the form of package tours, the tour operators are able to procure substantial discounts from carriers, hoteliers, etc. and offer their package deals at much lower rates. The profits of the tour operators and the success of his operations, however, depend on achieving of very high load factors for the aircraft and very high occupancy rates for the hotel. In this way, unit costs can be maintained sufficiently low to enable the tour operator to offer his package at a price which is often less than the cheapest available fare alone. A breakthrough in the business of tour operation came when airlines recognised that tour operation can fill the empty seats and introduced special fares for use exclusively by tour operators for combining into an inclusive tour.

The tour operator has thus emerged as the true manufacturer of the inclusive tour product packaged, standardised and mass-produced. The tour operator may sell this product directly to the public or through the channels of the retail travel agencies. It can be marketed successfully in the tourist generating countries to a mass market just because it is standardised, packaged and quality controlled. The product is therefore susceptible to the similar marketing techniques that are applied to the marketing of consumer goods.

Guiding Factors

The agent's role in handling a client is very important. Once a client enters the agency it becomes necessary for an agent to properly anticipate his needs and requirements. The client also has come with a predetermined notion about a destination he is visiting. WATA, the World Association of Travel Agencies, has prepared comprehensive guidelines for handling a client. These guidelines are based on the WATA Master-Key, an annual publication of the World Association of Travel Agencies. Updated and published yearly, the WATA Master-Key is a selectively comprehensive source of travel information. Individual agency tariffs given in the publication, represent the selling tool for members, incoming and outgoing services. Along with the tariffs the Master-Key gives a country description sheet containing a wealth of useful background information of a destination. In addition, the Master-Key also gives detailed information about some hotels located in important cities and tourist centres together with prevalent confidential tariffs and other relevant information for travel agencies.

The WATA Master-Key is a valuable reference material for travel agents. Its presentation makes it easy for the users to extract the information they need. The guidelines as enumerated in the Master-Key are as follows:

Sale of Tour : It should first be determined whether the client who wants to book a tour prefers to:

a. Join an escorted tour, or

b. Choose a FIT, combining leisure and activity according to his individual tastes and interests.

FIT/Your Relations with Client : If your client wants a "tailor made" tour, let him make the suggestions, without imposing your own views, on the following points:

Itinerary

1. Determine the cities to be visited.
2. Number of days (overnights) in each place.
3. Mode of transportation between cities.

4. Establish a rough time schedule, taking into consideration the time at his disposal.

Transportation

1. Air transport should be used when time is limited and for long distances.
2. Surface transportation should be recommended for shorter distances.
3. For trains, determine whether advanced reservation is necessary. Indicate stations where trains are to be changed.
4. Bus should be recommended in some countries, as it usually allows additional sightseeing.
5. When arranging timetables, remember that your client is on vacation, and therefore avoid early departures.

Hotel Accommodation

Category of Hotels : Examine with your client which category of hotel he wants to stay at-Deluxe, First Class, Standard or Economy class. It is preferable that he is accommodated in a maximum rate room; however, if he must consider the cost, then rather suggest a lower grade hotel with best available room.

Type of Rooms : Examine whether your client wishes a special room on a special floor, with or without bath/ shower, sea view, outside or inside, etc. Draw his attention to the fact that in high season a room with a bath may be difficult to obtain in some places. In some cases a double room for single occupancy can be suggested, a single room being often small or not well situated. If your client insists on having a particular room, he may have to pay a supplement.

Meals : Ask your client whether he wants to have accommodation on bed and breakfast, demi-pension or full pension basis. If accommodation is on bed and breakfast basis, keep in mind that in certain resorts, demi or full pension is compulsory.

Check-in Time: Remind your client that check-in time at hotels is usually after 12 noon. Immediate occupancy on early morning arrivals can only be secured if the room is reserved for the previous night. If your client leaves late in the evening you may propose to him to pay for an additional night.

During periods of festivals, fairs or congresses, hotel space may not be available, rendering it necessary for your client to change the dates in those places; cabled hotel confirmation should, therefore, be suggested.

During periods, such as important festivals and events, a minimum stay of 5-7 days may be required. The same is applicable to some winter resorts, where a minimum stay of two weeks is required at Christmas and New Year.

Transfers

1. The need of transfers upon arrival or departure results from the fact that it is often difficult to find one's way at airport, piers or stations with which one is not familiar.
2. Transfers by agencies include interpreter meeting and assistance, accompanying clients (unless otherwise specified), porterage and transportation of 2 pieces of hand luggage per person between airport, station, bus or air terminal and hotels or vice versa, as well as tip to driver, but it does not include tip to hotel porter.
3. Type of vehicle varies according to cities, generally by private car or taxi/cab.
4. Airport transfers are naturally more expensive, but also the most convenient ones.

5. When opting for transfer from city air terminal, your client must know that there will be no assistance at the airport, that he will have to tip for baggage at the airport and pay for bus between the airport and the city terminal.
6. Bus Arrivals: Certain bus companies stop at the major hotels to drop or collect clients, the disadvantage of this being the clients' dependence on time schedules and waiting for his turn to be dropped off. In addition, it will be necessary for the client to contact the local agency if other services are not to be provided in that city.

Sightseeing/Excursions/Tours

1. The advantage of arranging sightseeing in advance is that your client does not have to waste his time, queuing up in the local agency. Also, a balance can be established in advance between leisure time and sightseeing, as well as for tours of the city and countryside.
2. Motor Coach Tours : Apart from the economic viewpoint, there is the advantage of meeting other travellers, but clients have to arrange their own transportation to meeting points, as pick-up is very seldom done on motorcoach tours.
3. Private Car Tours : Your client is picked up at the hotel, has the choice of time of departure and can stop wherever he likes, but this is the most expensive solution. In some places there are regular private car tours, or else sightseeing can be done on a seat-in-car basis.
4. Hire of Private Car with Chauffeur

   (a) City hire-must be recommended to deluxe clients, whose time is limited between trains, boats or planes, or who already know the city and want to see only special places or go shopping. Since very often the chauffeur cannot act as a guide, a private guide will be needed for sightseeing.

(b) Touring hire-if a private car is used for travelling from one city to another, local guides in each place will be sufficient. Distance covered daily should not exceed 250 km. Client's attention has to be drawn to the fact that he will have to pay for empty run of car (return to point of departure). The full daily basic charge is due, even if the vehicle is picked up in the evening.

5. Motor Launch Tours/Boats Trips : The same applies here as for motor coach tours. Deluxe clients will be picked up at the hotel by private car and driven to embarkation pier.

6. Self-driven cars can also be provided when clients fill the necessary conditions and, if wanted, a local guide can be placed at their disposal.

Music Festival, Theatre and Concert Tickets

Clients must be told that advance reservation is necessary. Confirmation of requested tickets cannot be guaranteed and tickets are not refundable unless they can be resold.

Land Arrangements : On the basis of all details furnished by your clients, it will enable you to make an estimate of the land arrangements.

Transatlantic/Pacific Transportation : To the land arrangements, the cost of flight/boat tickets for Transatlantic/ Pacific transportation has to be added.

Cost Price : Items a and b above give you the cost price.

Selling Price : In order to obtain the selling price you have to add your handling fees or mark-up, as well as a margin safeguarding any possible increase.

Suggested Itinerary

(a) A suggested itinerary should be drafted of what has been agreed with your client and submitted to him, together with the final price. The accompanying letter should clearly specify what is included in the price:

1. Price and type of land arrangements.
2. Price and class of air/sea/rail tickets, indicating that they are subject to change without notice.
3. The agency's conditions regarding handling charge , cancellation fees, possible deposit request, etc.

(b) It should also point out what is NOT included, such as cost of passport, visa, gratuities, tips to hotel porters, beverages, laundry, taxes (government, landing, embarkation), etc.

(c) Acceptance of suggested itinerary should be requested to enable you to proceed with reservation, and a deposit should be asked.

Your Relation with Service Suppliers : Reservation Procedures

(a) Once you are in possession of the client's agreement you can start reservations with carriers and hotels.

(b) In case your client requests only hotel reservations in a few places, it is advisable to make the reservations directly with the hotels.

(c) However, if transfer, sightseeing or other services are also requested, then it is preferable to go through the local agent, who is in a better position to replace a hotel by a similar one, in case of full occupancy.

Transfers : Due to frequent changes in time schedules and/or due to changes your client may require, it is NOT advisable to send transfer requests earlier than one month prior to final documentation. An exception can be made if a special service is required and rate confirmation is needed.

Transfers should be requested by vouchers, indicating the following items:

(a) Full name of client(s) and number of passengers (for a child or an aged person give their age also).

(b) Date of transfer.

(c) Full description (indicate type of car, name of airport, city air terminal or station, exact flight or train number and arrival/ departure time).

(d) Name of hotel the client is staying at.

(e) Town and date of issue.

(f) If you do not have the rate of a service, request the rate of confirmation on the voucher copies.

Transportation : Whenever possible, obtain all tickets for rail, bus, boat, cruise, sleeping cars, etc., that may be required locally from agencies of foreign railroads, bus companies, steamship lines, etc.

HOTEL ACCOMMODATION

1. Depending on the time you have, hotel reservations can be made by reservation requests, by telex or cable (give paid reply), through hotel representatives, or through a WATA office. If you reserve through a a hotel representative or WATA office, their conditions should be respected.
2. Once you have a hotel confirmation, issue a voucher for re- confirmation, indicating the following items:

(a) Full name of client(s) and number of persons (for a child or an aged person give their age also).

(b) Type of room.

(c) Arrival and departure date, time of arrival and flight/ train number.

(d) Meal conditions - clearly indicate whether rooms only, bed and breakfast (Continental or American/English), half or full pension.

(e) Always mention on hotel vouchers: "All taxes and service charges included".

(f) Method of payment-indicate who will pay the bill. If the client settles the bill directly with the hotel, even when a deposit has been sent, hotels do not always pay a commission.

(g) Always ask for a re-confirmation of the rate on the voucher copies.

3. If the best room is required, it should be determined as DELUXE, and a 10 per cent supplement foreseen.

4. If a suite is required, it can be estimated a 2½ times the normal tariff.

5. Whenever necessary, an extra night is to be foreseen for early arrival or late departure. Indicate on voucher early a.m. arrival the following day or request additional night or day use, advising the exact departure time.

6. In case of split stays at the same hotel, a separate voucher should be issued for each day.

Sightseeing/Excursions/Tours

The same applies as for transfers - regular sightseeing tours should not be requested earlier than one month prior to the final documentation, except when a special service is required (e.g., sightseeing starting at airport) or for excursions/tours of two or more days' duration.

1. Sightseeing/Excursions/Tours should be requested for WATA affiliates by vouchers, indicating the following items:
   (a) Full name of client(s) and number of persons (for a child or an aged person give their age also).
   (b) Date of sightseeing/excursions/tours.
   (c) Reference number of tour (if given), tour designation and title.
   (d) By private car or by regular scheduled motor coach.
   (e) For regular tours, give time and place of departure for private car tours, indicate "pick-up at hotel".
   (f) Name of hotel client is staying at.
   (g) Town and date of issue.
   (h) In case a complete description does not appear in the agent's tariff, ask for additional information and rate confirmation.
2. If your client wants to start a sightseeing tour from airport or station, add transfer-rate to sightseeing rate.

Chauffeur Driven Car Hire

1. If private car hire with chauffeur is required, it has to be reserved in advance on the basis of rates quoted in the Master-Key. If rates are not given, apply to the agency for rates and details.
2. For requests, issue voucher, indicating the following details:

(a) Full name of client(s) and number of passengers.

(b) Type of car (year of construction if available).

(c) For city hire : Date and time of beginning of hire, length of hire or time of termination.

(d) For touring hire: Date of beginning and termination of hire, starting time of hire and termination point, as well as stopovers.

(e) Special requests, such as automatic cars, air conditioning, luggage, rack, etc.

(f) Name of hotel client is staying at.

3. City and Touring hire must be issued on separate vouchers, as tariffs and minimum daily averages are not the same. Also, if more than one day city hire is required issue one voucher for each day.

4. Touring rate is established on the basis of a reliable map. Ten per cent of total mileage should be added for detours. If there are overnight stops, an additional 20 miles should be foreseen for possible use of car during the stay in city.

5. For empty runs, it should be noted that the law does not authorise chauffeurs to drive more than 310 miles/500 km per day, therefore, the total distance should be divided by this authorised maximum to reckon the number of chauffeur's overnights to be added to the touring rate.

6. For chauffeur's accommodation, the rate appearing in the tariff has to be multiplied by the number of days the car has been used (special rates if outside the country).

Self-Driven Cars : If given, use rates appearing in the WATA Master-Key, otherwise, apply to the agency or consult Hertz, Avis, etc., for details and rates, whenever so indicated.

WATA Master-Key is a valuable document for a travel agent. The guidelines given in 'key' make the job of a travel agent a lot easier. As a comprehensive source of travel information it facilitates the work of a travel agent. The destination profiles provide a wealth of background information not only for a travel agent but also for a traveller. The 'key' is updated every year making it a valuable reference material.

IATA Accredition : Travel agents are the marketplace intermediaries responsible for selling the services of airlines worldwide. Considering the role and importance of air transport which is at the heart of travel and tourism selling, its services becomes the key motivation for engaging in travel agency business. Therefore, the importance of IATA approval for a travel agency is essential to enable it to sell the services of airlines.

For setting up a travel agency business there are no legal requirements. In some countries, however, governments exercise some kind of a licensing control over agencies. Most principals license the sale of their services through the issue of an agency contract, or agency agreement. In the absence of such a contract or an agreement, a travel agency will not get any commission from selling the services on behalf of the principal. The income of a travel agent is derived only from a commission which he receives from the principal after selling their services.

A licence is required by a travel agency for a commission to be payable on the sale of services of air carriers who are members of the International Air Transport Association. Domestic air services are, however, exempted from this. Most airlines want to sell their services worldwide but cannot do so on their own as it is not economically viable for them to set up extensive network of sales offices in every city of the world. It is the travel agents who are the marketplace intermediaries who make the sale of the services of the airlines possible worldwide through their own network.

As IATA travel makes up a substantial proportion of a total sale of a travel agency turnover, it is important for the travel agent who wishes to offer his clients the full range of travel services to obtain the necessary IATA approval or appointment.

IATA-Controlled Approval : The travel agency approval of IATA is controlled by its Agency Administration Board. This Board is made up of a number of IATA members operating from a particular country. Before approval is granted by IATA, a travel agency has to fulfil certain conditions. The most important condition is the demonstration by an agency of its financial soundness or financial standing. It has to prove that it has sufficient finances to settle the accounts of various airlines whose business it is handling. Another condition which an agency has to fulfil is to ensure the suitability and security of its premises. The premises of a travel agency are to be centrally located preferably in the centre of the town in a commercial district having proper security. The security aspect is very important as the agency has to keep the ticket stock of various airlines and this is quite expensive.

Proficiency of the staff of a travel agency is another important aspect which is considered by IATA before giving an approval. The staff has to be professionally trained in the handling of airlines business. IATA in association with UFTAA conducts the International Travel Agents Training Programme to meet the growing demand for a professionally trained manpower for the travel industry. The IATA-UFTAA training programme operates under the authority of the Passenger Agency Training Board. IATA's Agency Training Services (ATS) located in Geneva (Switzerland) is responsible for the general administration of the programme.

In the field, the training programme is administered by a Local Coordinator who is responsible for the promotion of the training courses, the distribution of the training materials and the organisation of the examinations. The Local Coordinator is provided by the local IATA Agency Services, the National Airlines or the National Travel Agents Association in a particular country.

The IATA-UFTAA training courses have been designed primarily for travel professionals who work in IATA accredited travel agencies and whose main task is to sell international air transportation on behalf of IATA member airlines. The agents' staff can demonstrate proficiency by completing an IATA/ UFTAA (passenger) training course.

The applicant's ability to generate new business is another requirement to be taken into consideration by IATA before considering an application for approval. This is to ensure that an agent is capable of generating new business in the market and has sufficient contacts to do so. To sum up, any travel agency, in order to get IATA approval for selling the services of IATA airlines worldwide, has to ensure the following:

(i) Financial standing

(ii) Suitability of the premises

(iii) Security for control of ticket stock

(iv) Proficiency of the staff

(v) Ability to generate new business

After considering the above aspects and if the IATAs Agency Administration Board is satisfied, necessary IATA approval is accorded to an agency. Once approved, a Passenger Sales Agreement is issued and a numeric ticket validation code is provided which will be stamped on all tickets issued by that IATA-approved agent. IATA approval enables the agent to do business on behalf of all IATA members. It enables the agent to sell the services of all IATA member airlines throughout the world. The entire process of getting IATA approval can be quite time-consuming and lengthy and in the meantime agents applying for IATA approval are expected to generate business without getting any commissions.

Additional Approvals : In addition to the IATA approval which is basic for a travel agency, there are certain other approvals/recognitions required for running a travel agency. These approvals, however, will depend on the extent of activities and range of services which a particular agency would like to offer to its clients. For instance, in order to make commissionable sales on the services of railways, domestic airlines services and other principals such as car hire companies, shipping and cruise services, necessary approval is to be obtained. These approvals will enable travel agents to sell services on behalf of these principals with remuneration. In case a travel agency is an IATA-approved agent, or a member of the National Travel Agents Association, obtaining approvals for most of other principals becomes largely a formality.

Travel and Trade Associations

Formation of associations by independent firms in a particular trade or a group of industries is primarily done with a view to protecting the interests of its members. Trade Organisations are voluntary bodies formed by individual firms belonging to a particular trade not only to protect but also to advance the common interests of their members. The main objective of forming an association by independent firms is to get strong representations which act as channels of communication with the government and other organised groups to further the interests of their members. In almost all disciplines, members sharing similar interests or complementing each other's interests in some way or other have formed organisations/associations.

The ever-increasing importance of the tourism sector and the increase in the growth in its volume over the years have resulted in the formation of associations in this sector. Secondly, the ever-increasing international character of the modern day tourism and the growing influence of international agencies in various fields have also influenced the growth of international cooperations in the field of tourism. All these developments in turn have brought together members of the travel associations at national, regional and international levels collectively to further their trade interests. Different producers and sellers of various tourist services like tour operators, travel agents, hotel companies, airline companies, ground operators, etc., have formed associations of their members.

The scope of discussion in this chapter is limited to the associations of travel agents and tour operators. These associations today have assumed great importance and provide a platform to their members where ideas are exchanged and topics of mutual interest discussed and solutions arrived at. They provide services like information, assistance and advice in the conduct of their business to their members. The various associations in the field of tourism can take different forms. Broadly, the following five forms can be identified:

(i) Those based on the education and training needs of the industry. These may include professional bodies like Hotel and Catering Management Association, Travel and Tourism Management Association which are primarily concerned with the training and educational standards of personnel working in hotel and travel agencies.

(ii) Those which are concerned with the sectoral interests of their members. They include the National Associations of Travel Agents and Tour Operators. Each country has such associations. For instance, the American Society of Travel Agents (ASTA), the Australian Federation of Travel Agents (AFTA), the Association of British Travel Agents (ABTA), the Japan Association of Travel Agents (JATA), the Indian Association of Travel Agents (IATA), the Swiss Travel Agents Association, the German Travel Agencies' Association, etc.

(iii) Those which are responsible for developing, promoting and facilitating tourism among a particular region. These regional organisations draw their membership from public or private sector organisations dealing with tourism and sharing a common interest in the promotion and development or marketing of a specific tourism geographical area or a region. This area may represent a region, a state, a country or a resort. The membership is opened to groups or organisations, both in public and private sectors, rather than individuals, such as Pacific Area Travel Association (PATA), etc.

(iv) Those which are concerned with the promotion and development of tourism globally. These organisations deal with all the aspects of tourism. The rapid expansion in tourism activity globally was responsible for creating a need for world bodies to deal with tourism issues at the government level. The World Tourism Organisation (WTO) is one such global tourism organisation representing public sector tourism from most countries of the world.

(v) Those which are responsible for promoting and furthering interests of specific trade groups in the travel industry, like travel agents, and tour operators at the global level. Unlike the sectoral trade association of travel agents and tour operators, these have international impact. They play an important role in representing the common interests of travel agents and tour operators worldwide in crucial international issues like negotiation of travel agency commission rates with International Air Transport Association (IATA). Universal Federation of Travel Agents Association (UFTAA) and the World Association of Travel Agencies (WATA) are such associations. Both UFTAA and WATA play an important role in representing the interests of travel agents worldwide. The following pages will discuss in detail the roles and functions of these two international organisations of travel agents.

Universal Federation of Travel Agents Association (UFTAA) : Universal Federation of Travel Agents Association (UFTAA), an important organisation of travel agents on a worldwide basis, was founded in Rome in November, 1966 by the merger of the International Federation of Travel Agencies (IFTA) and the Universal Organisation of Travel Agents' Associations (UOTAA). The General Secretariat of UFTAA is located in Monaco.

The membership of the Federation consists of the National, Travel Agents' Associations from most of the countries in the world. Today it represents over 33,000 travel agencies globally. National Travel Agents Associations are the full members of UFTAA. The membership of the Federation is split into nine regions each covering a group of countries.

List of Countries of which the National Association is a Member of UFTAA

Algeria	Guatemala	Norway
Argentina	Hungary	Pakistan
Australia	Hong Kong	Paraguay

Algeria	**Guatemala**	**Norway**
Austria	India	Peru
Barbados	Indonesia	Philippines
Belgium	Iraq	Poland
Bolivia	Ireland	Portugal
Brazil	Israel	Puerto Rico
Bulgaria	Italy	Senegal
Canada	Ivory Coast	Singapore
Chile	Japan	South Africa
Colombia	Jordan	South Korea
Costa Rica	Kenya	Spain
Cuba	Kuwait	Sri Lanka
Cyprus	Lebanon	Sweden
Czech Republic	Malaysia	Sudan
Cont....		
Dominican	Malawi	Syria
Denmark	Malta	Thailand
Egypt	Mexico	Trinidad and Tobago
Ecuador	Mauritius	Tunisia
El Salvador	Monaco	Turkey
Finland	Morocco	Uruguay
France	Nepal	Venezuela
Germany	Netherlands	Zaire

Algeria	Guatemala	Norway
Ghana	New Zealand	Zambia
Greece	Nigeria	Zimbabwe

The Aims of the Federation : The following are the main aims of the federation :

(i) To act as the negotiating body with the various branches of tourism and travel industry on behalf of its members and also in the interest of the public;

(ii) To ensure for all travel agents through their national associations the maximum degree of cohesion and understanding, prestige and public recognition, advancement of the member's interest and protection from legislation and legal points of view; and

(iii) To offer to its member all the necessary professional and technical advice and assistance in matters concerning their trade.

UFTAA provides several advantages to its members which include the right to reproduce the symbol on the stationery, information service on all matters of legal or professional nature, free of charge assistance by its Legal Department for the recovery of outstanding debts, arbitration services for litigations between a member agency and a hotel company in different countries, etc.

The Annual General Assembly of UFTAA is the policymaking body. The Assembly decides on the general policy of the Federation and makes recommendations on any matter within its competence. The Board of Directors, consisting of Directors elected from candidates proposed by National Member Associations handle the routine business of the Federation. The Executive Committee is responsible for handling day-to-day activities and also urgent matters. The UFTAA world congress which normally takes place annually is the advisory body of the Federation. The world congress is open to UFTAA registered agents and enterprises, UFTAA individual members, suppliers of services and regional, national and international public authorities.

UFTAA claims to have a series of achievements since its inception in the year 1966. Prominent among its achievements is its collaboration with the International Rail Union resulting in obtaining increased commission on several railway networks, creation of professional training courses and introduction of Rail inclusive Tours. With regard to air transport, the cooperation between the Federation and IATA over a number of years has resulted in the raising of commission, introduction of an overriding commission, 50 per cent reduction for the spouses of travel agents and creation of international correspondence courses for the training of agency sales staff. In the sphere of hotel industry, the federation, following negotiations with the International Hotel Association has created an international convention, setting down regulations for booking, and cancellation fees. A court of arbitration to settle disputes between hotels and travel agents located in different countries has also been created.

World Association of Travel Agencies (WATA) : WATA, the World Association of Travel Agencies, is another important worldwide association representing travel agencies. Founded in the year 1949, WATA is a non-profit organisation created by independent travel agents for the benefit of all travel agencies around the world. The Association has over 200 members from 175 cities in 80 countries. The headquarters of WATA are located in Geneva, Switzerland.

The basic idea of WATA is to bring together local travel agencies into an international network, so that every member is offered all the facilities and advantages of being associated with an international body in addition to enjoying local prominence. WATA is registered as an association under Swiss Civil Law, and is essentially a non-profit making organisation. Under its statutes, WATA and its members are required to assist one another.

The General Assembly of WATA held every year provides a forum for discussion of the Association's business and an opportunity to talk with fellow members. It enables members to have an exposure to new business and ideas applied successfully elsewhere. One day, before the General Assembly, the meetings of the Regional Assemblies are held which provide a chance to its members to discuss regional travel problems as well as the implementation on the regional level of the decisions taken by WATA governing bodies. The regions also have the possibility to submit to the General Assembly ideas and suggestions.

Advantages of a WATA Membership : The advantages of WATA membership include:

Guaranteed Payment of IHA Invoices : WATA headquarters guarantees payment of all invoices for services rendered by the International Hotel Association (IHA) hotel members to WATA members, up to a certain amount. In return, the IHA has requested its members to accept vouchers for individual clients issued by WATA members to be billed after the client's departure.

Internal Guarantee : Subject to certain conditions, unsettled services rendered by one WATA member agency to another, are paid by WATA headquarters.

WATA Standard Exchange Voucher : An agency's own exchange voucher bearing the WATA logo and the reference to the IHA/WATA agreement or the standard WATA exchange voucher printed by the headquarters with the name of agency, are widely accepted by hotels worldwide. In the majority of the cases, hotels accepting these vouchers will agree to bill the services after the departure of the clients without prepayment or deposit.

Membership List and Introduction Card : A small booklet listing all WATA members and their addresses is available for agencies to give to clients who go on extended trips, in case they need assistance and service en route. For specially important clients, a special introduction card is available for the members.

WATA Master-Key : Updated and published yearly, the WATA Master-Key is a comprehensive source of travel information. Individual WATA agency tariffs represent an invaluable selling tool for members' incoming and outgoing services. Master-Key carries the tariffs of WATA members offering incoming services. A standard presentation makes it easy for users to extract the information they need. Along with the tariffs is a country description sheet provided by the respective National Tourist Offices containing a wealth of background information.

WATA Circular Letters for Latest Developments : This internal newsletter keeps members abreast of new developments in WATA. It also gives members an opportunity to describe special activities of their own.

WATA's Overriding Commission : A supplementary commission of 5 per cent is allowed between members, on prices published in WATA Master-Key for transfers, sightseeing, excursions, tours and chauffeur-driven car hire.

WATA Membership Categories

Full Members : Membership in WATA is open to any travel agency, preferably privately-owned, which can prove a sound financial structure, adheres to the highest professional ethics expected in the industry and enjoys prominent standing in the local community.

All WATA members have the same rights, privileges and obligations within the association. Individual members are grouped into three sub-categories depending on the scope of their activities, as follows:

(1) Agencies offering both outgoing and incoming services.

(2) Agencies offering outgoing activities only.

(3) Agencies offering incoming service only.

Associate Members : A travel agency may apply to become an associate member. This category offers the possibility to become a WATA associate member for a trial period of 2 years. The associate members have the same rights and obligations as the full members but the fees are generally reduced.

Allied Members : A category open to hotels, airlines, shipping lines and car hire companies. The aim of this category is to develop the business relations between the members and their partners. Allied members may attend the WATA General Assembly, they will be listed in the WATA publications, receive all WATA publications and circulate letters and have the right to display on all their printed matter, the WATA logo created for this category. They have no voting right nor can they be elected to the WATA governing bodies. Both UFTAA and WATA are playing a valuable role in representing the interests of travel agents worldwide. In addition to the above two international travel associations representing travel agents, there are some important national travel agents organisations like the American Society of Travel Agents (ASTA) which has influence beyond the confines of USA. The American Society of Travel Agents draws its membership not only from travel agents and principals within the country but also from principals throughout the world who have interest in promoting overseas tourism from United States to their country.

The American Society of Travel Agents (ASTA) : American Society of Travel Agents (ASTA) is the leading professional society of travel agents in the USA. The world's largest professional travel trade association, ASTA was established in New York in the year 1931. Originally named the American Steamship and Tourist Agent's Association, the present name was adopted in the year 1944. The Society was established to foster programmes for the advancement of the travel agency industry, promote ethical practices and provide a public forum for travel agents. It has now over 25,000 members and is the only organisation representing all segments of the travel industry. The membership consists of travel agents, carriers, hotels, etc.

Purpose : The purpose of ASTA is the promotion and advancement of the interests of the travel agency industry and the safeguarding of the travelling public against fraud, misrepresentation and other unethical practices. The Society maintains legal representation and also a Government Affairs office in Washington, D.C. to provide direct contact with the Federal Government and the regulatory agencies in the travel and transportation field, and to protect the legitimate interests of travel agents.

Services : ASTA's services to travel agents also benefit the general public. Such activities include sponsorship of frequent conferences on travel matters, involving airlines, steamship companies, agents, municipal and government officials, and other interested parties; discussions with airlines on fare structures and travel destinations; research studies into traveller preferences; close cooperation with various city, state and government agencies across the country in travel-oriented matters, assistance to all agencies across the country in travel-oriented matters; assistance to all levels of government consumerism departments in upgrading standards of service to travellers.

The American Society of Travel Agents is primarily the trade association of the travel agency industry. There are more than 25,000 members in the Society covering all segments of the travel industry. Out of the total membership of 25,000 over 14,000 are travel agents in the United States of America and Canada. In addition to travel agents, there are allied members representing airlines, railways, hotels, government tourist offices, etc. The Society has a membership in over 140 countries all over the world. In order to qualify for the membership of the Society, an applicant must be in the business of travel under its present ownership or control for a minimum period of three years.

Membership : There are two basic classifications of membership-Active and Allied. Active members are year-round travel agents or tour operators. Allied members include airlines and steamship companies, railroad, bus lines, car rental firms, hotels, resorts, government tourist offices and other organisations regularly engaged in the travel industry or associated industries.

ASTA has over 2,500 travel agency members outside the USA and Canada. All are engaged in travel agency operations on a year-round basis and have been in business for at least three consecutive years. The international roster has its own elected governors and actively participates in all phases of Society meetings. International members come from Algeria, Bolivia, Sri Lanka, Denmark, Ethiopia, Fiji Island, Ghana, India, Iran, Japan, the Netherlands, Portugal, South Africa and Sweden.

ASTA World Travel Congress : The year's foremost meeting place is the ASTA World Travel Congress. The Congress is the single most important meeting held annually in the travel industry and the programme includes workshops, seminars, business meetings, film presentations, and social events. Members from throughout the world travel industry participate, give talks, lead discussion groups and conduct sessions. The ASTA World Travel Congress has been the platform for launching many important and beneficial education programmes for agents. The Congress grants Travel Hall of Fame awards, an honour given to those whose careers have made long standing impacts on the development and expansion of the travel industry and tourism. The awards are given every year to outstanding members. ASTA consists of the following departments:

(a) Policy implementation

(b) Administration

(c) Industry relations

(d) Membership relations

(e) Communication

The members of the society derive various advantages which include education and training. ASTA has a comprehensive list of travel courses and seminars which are attended by its members. The society also offers professional training courses to senior travel agency personnel. Various research papers and newsletters are brought out from the Society's headquarters for use of its members.

ASTA Chapters : The society has 28 chapters in the United States of America and Canada and another 28 chapters overseas. Each chapter has elected officers and appointed committees. There is a National Board of Directors which establishes policies of the Society. Every two years a new President and Chairman of the Board are elected by Active Members. Day-to-day activities of the Society are looked after by a professional staff which works under the guidance of an Executive Vice-President who, in fact, is the Chief Operating Officer of the society and makes recommendations on policy matters to the Board and Executive Board. The Vice-President directs the headquarters staff in providing a broad programme of services and facilities to ASTA's membership and carrying on the day-to-day business of the Society. ASTA world headquarters are located in New York City, USA.

Indian Scenario : As long back as in the year 1954, the Government of India was aware of the important role which the travel agents were to play in the development of tourism. It was recognised by the Government that tourists who visit a foreign country often prefer to secure the services of travel agents who assist them in order to make best use of time and money at their disposal. The government felt that many a time unauthorised persons offer themselves as agents and in return fail to render satisfactory services, and even exploit the ignorance of the tourists for their personal benefit. With a view to curb this the government evolved a system of granting recognition to travel agents. The rules for recognition were as follows:

(i) No firm shall be granted recognition unless it has been engaged actively in handling tourist traffic for at least one year before the date of the application.

(ii) Firms granted recognition shall be entitled to such right and privileges as may be granted by the government from time to time and shall abide by several terms and conditions of recognition.

(iii) Firms granted recognition shall undertake to maintain an office under the charge of full time members of their staff who should, apart from issuing rail tickets, be in a position to give up to date and accurate information regarding transport and accommodation facilities, currency and customs regulations and general information about travel, etc.

(iv) The recognition may be extended for the whole of the country or be limited to a particular region.

(v) Firms granted recognition shall undertake to employ only guides approved by the Ministry of Tourism.

(vi) All recognised firms shall furnish yearly statement of their activities and such other information in regard to the volume of tourist traffic actually handled and other relevant matters.

(vii) The decision of the government in the matter of recognition shall be final and it reserves the right to cancel or withdraw it at any time.

Subsequently, following clauses were also added:

(i) The recognition to be granted by Ministry of Tourism shall not automatically entitle the firm to be appointed agents for the sale of rail tickets by the Ministry of Railways (Railway Board). The agencies thus recognised shall apply separately to the Railway Board.

(ii) Firms seeking recognition as travel agents should have a minimum paid-up capital of rupees one hundred thousand.

(iii) Applications for grant of recognition by the Ministry of Tourism will be considered only if the firm:

(a) is approved by the IATA;

(b) has licence to book foreign passages issued by the Reserve Bank of India;

(c) has the approval of the Ministry of External Affairs to handle travel documents and to deal with passport offices;

(d) is registered under the Local Shops and Establishment Act.

The recognition is now granted by the Ministry of Tourism in the Ministry of Tourism and Culture. The application for grant of recognition is to be made in the prescribed form and is to be addressed to the Director General, Ministry of Tourism who is the authority empowered to grant such recognition.

Travel Agents Association of India (TAAI) : The travel agents decided to form an association on all-India basis as long back as in the year 1952, when an All India Travel Agents Association was established. The main objective of the association is to safeguard and protect the interests of its members by way of having a constant dialogue with the concerned government agencies. The annual convention of the association is attended by a large number of representatives from travel trade both government as well as non-government. Important matters related with the promotion of product are discussed in these conventions. The Travel Agents Association of India has its registered office in Mumbai and regional offices in Kolkata, Delhi and Chennai. The association publishes a monthly magazine *Travel News* for of its members.

The vital role played by the travel agents in the growth and development of tourism in the country and its promotion is recognised by all segments of the travel industry. The government works in close collaboration with them not only in India but abroad as well, encouraging them to plan and organize package tours for various destinations in India. In suitable cases, the Ministry of Tourism recommends the foreign exchange to travel agents to enable them to open their branch offices abroad. The ministry has also instituted a special tourism award which is given every year to the agency earning the maximum amount of foreign exchange.

6

ROLE OF TRAVEL AGENCIES IN TOURISM PROMOTION

Among travel agents, there are the *Wholesalers* and *Retailers.* The wholesalers develop package tours to many a destination and sell them either directly to travellers, or through retail travel agents— small travel agencies operating in each country. Retailers get a ten per cent commission from wholesalers for every package tour sold. The retailers need not make any arrangement for their customers themselves—that is the responsibility of the wholesalers who are in touch with hotels and travel agencies overseas, if it is an overseas package, or within the country if it is a domestic package, for making what in travel agents' terminology is called 'ground arrangements'. The tour operators who receive guests and handle arrangements in the host country are called 'Inbound tour operators'. They service the inbound travellers from foreign countries. Those who promote tours to foreign destinations are called

'Outbound tour operators', while those who operate tours only within their own country, are called 'Domestic tour operators'. Several of them combine both types of businesses. Tour operation is a complicated business—wheels within wheels, each doing its job to make travel trouble-free for the tourists.

There is a thin line between the different kinds of travel agencies—big travel agencies often combine all the functions including retail selling. They have several branches in a country. Sometimes they act as wholesalers and permit other travel agencies also to retail their tour packages. Wholeselling is a popular business in countries like the USA where one company may move as many as half a million people in a year. In India, it is not so common as yet. Often, wholesalers have their retail outlets as well. With the taking over of large Indian companies like Sita World Travel by Kuonis, a multinational travel company, wholeselling will be a big business in future.

Types of Travel Agencies

Basically, there are two types of travel agencies: the general travel agency and the specialised travel agency. The general travel agency is a small organisation (two to ten employees) that deals with almost all types of travel and offers nearly every type of travel-related service. The specialised travel agency is a fairly large operation and may specialise in one form of travel, or travel service to a group or a community. In India, most travel agencies belong to the category of general travel agencies.

The specialised travel agencies—not very common in India— may specialise in corporate and commercial accounts, exclusively dealing with business travel, organising air tickets, arranging hotel accommodation, car rentals, etc., for corporate executives. The other areas of specialisation are ship or cruise travel, outbound travel, specially in packaging and marketing overseas holidays, organising and promoting conferences and conventions, and creating and catering to an incentive travel market, etc. Some travel agencies confine their business to developing and marketing domestic tours only. This is an excellent business in developed countries and is now becoming profitable in India too.

Travel Agency Commissions

Surprisingly, most travel agencies do not charge anything from their clients for their professional services. They survive on commission given by their principals, i.e., airlines, hotels, motels, railways, car rental companies, bus and insurance companies, etc. Where they do not get commissions, they may make a service charge. For instance, the Indian Railways do not give commissions to travel agents. So, a travel agency will add its service charge if a client wants them to buy rail-ticket. However, Indian Railways makes an exception. They permit ten per cent commission to travel agents selling *Indrail Passes* to foreign visitors against foreign currency. They also offer the same commission on sale of Palace on Wheels' tickets.

Commissions to travel agents vary from country to country, depending on the competitive situation. For instance, commissions go up to fifteen per cent and more in the USA where the international airlines are free to offer any commission to make a sale. There is virtually no ceiling on payment of commission due to the policy of deregulation followed by the US Government. But now the airlines are getting wiser and some of them have put a ceiling or 'Caps' as they call it. It has made travel agencies less profitable. The scene is changing due to tight economic situation of airlines.

In India, we follow the IATA norms—seven per cent commission on international tickets. Till recently, Indian Airlines followed their own rules. They had the monopoly and paid a low four per cent commission. With the entry of private airlines, Indian Airlines now pays five per cent commission—the same as the private airlines. Now, the Government has added its ten per cent tax on the total value of the domestic air ticket, which a travel agent is required to collect. No commission is paid to him by the Government for this service. Tax goes to the Government coffers.

Promotion

Since travel agency business is highly competitive, the management of the agency must have a comprehensive marketing plan to facilitate sale of its services.

Under the broad term 'marketing', promotion means all the activities undertaken to promote a business and its products and services. It includes the projection of a proper image of the agency and creation of demands for the services of the travel agency. It can be done by personal contacts, through a sales force and advertising.

A travel agent sells his services. Sometimes, there may be some malfunctioning somewhere in the long chain of travel, not necessarily due to the fault of the agent. It may be the fault of an airline which did not operate a service on time, or of the hotel which did not honour a reservation due to overbooking. But, the travel agent gets the blame from his clients. It is a business full of tensions. There is an interesting story of a travel agent who died and was face to face with St. Peter. He was trembling and expecting to be confined to hell because he never had time to pray in his lifetime. St. Peter asked,

"What was your profession on earth?"

"A travel agent, sir."

St. Peter gave a benevolent smile and ordered, "Let him go to heaven. The poor fellow had enough of hell on earth at the hands of his clients."

Role in International Tourism

Travel agencies play a key role in promoting international tourism. In India, only twenty-five per cent of incoming business is handled by established travel agencies—mostly groups. Other visitors make independent arrangements. But they should have a larger share and should be helped by the Government to handle more inbound business. The travel agents of India have a good reputation overseas and are known for their efficiency, reliability and hospitality.

The National Committee on Tourism set up by the Government of India, underlined the importance of travel agencies in marketing Indian tourism overseas. The Committee said:

Considering that the travel trade industry is an important link in the total tourism chain, we recommend that the industry should be extended suitable incentives to help improve its performance. We believe that the activities of the travel trade are in the nature of export services, earning foreign exchange as they do. As such, the industry needs to be given selected fiscal and monetary incentives which are already available to the export industry.

Some concessions were extended to travel agents earning foreign exchange in the budget presented by Dr Manmohan Singh, for the year 1992 - 93. More concessions have been added by the Finance Minister in 1997 and subsequently in 2000.

The Committee suggested that travel agents should get the same concessions for earning foreign exchange as the hotel industry. The plants and machinery of the travel agents are cars, coaches, camping, sports and skiing equipment...low customs duty on such equipment should be levied as for project imports. According to an American Express Travel Agency Survey in India, corporate business for travel agents in India is increasing at the rate of ten per cent annually (American Express Survey, 1996).

No wonder, therefore, the rate of IATA approved travel agencies folding up in India is one of the lowest, in fact, negligible.

Changing Pattern of Travel Agencies

The travel agency scene in the world, specially in the developed countries, is fast changing. Deregulation of civil aviation in the USA, followed by several other countries, brought in a plethora of reduced airfares and tempting commission structures. Lower airfares resulted in expanded business and higher commissions for travel agents. Business has never been so good. In the USA, membership of IATA is no longer necessary to claim commission from IATA or other scheduled carriers. America has set up its own Air Transport Association (ATA) which works closely with IATA. Agent members of ATC—a division of ATA of America— are as good as IATA agents and IATA has endorsed them.

Many Governments including those of the USA, UK, Japan and Singapore, have enacted legislation regulating the working of travel agencies to protect the consumers. The regulations insist that new travel agencies will have trained staff, minimum capitalisation and consumer protection insurance, etc. There have been instances of large travel agencies declaring bankruptcies, while hundreds of their clients were travelling in many countries—leaving them high and dry as airlines refused to honour their tickets. In India, there is no legislation regulating travel agencies or protecting travellers. The newly set-up of Consumers Forums can, however, take note of complaints against travel agents.

Attracted by new opportunities in expanding travel business, the number of IATA-approved travel agencies has doubled in ten years, from thirty thousand in 1980 to over sixty thousand in 2000, according to an IATA report.

Statistics pertaining to the travel agency business in the USA are mind-boggling. In 1995, travel agencies in the USA wrote a record US$45 billion in airlines ticketing—commission payments amounted to US$4 billion. In India, statistics pertaining to legal payment in the form of commissions are seldom available— airlines are secretive about it as part of it is often paid under the table. The Indian Airlines which has no reason to be secretive about commission is also reluctant to part with this information in an attempt to expand their area of direct sales at the cost of travel agents.

Overall, approved Indian travel agents sell more than sixty per cent of domestic and seventy-five per cent of international tickets. The rest of the selling is done either directly by the Airlines or through their General Sales Agents (GSAs), which have mushroomed everywhere. GSAs are normally appointed by an airline at a place where there are no IATA agents. A GSA sells tickets of only one airline which he represents and operates his office as the Airlines' own office, entitling him to a higher commission. Over the years, GSAs in India have become an outlet for price-cutting by airlines to beat the competition. They have become experts in cross-border selling—selling across the area of their jurisdiction. Air India, the national carrier, has its GSA in New Delhi where there are more than a score of IATA agents, not setting a very good example for foreign carriers. IATA agents are often hostile to the institution of GSAs because they know that this is a way of taking away their legitimate business from them, by their own principals—the international airlines.

New Developments

Deregulation of airlines in the USA in the eighties, enabled airlines to offer any fare to travel agents or consumers. It has led to two new developments in the travel agency distribution system. One is the emergence of *Consolidators*—business organisations which buy airlines and cruise tickets in bulk at special rates from the principals and offer these at discounted prices to travel agents. The other is *Consortium* or *Co-ops.*

A Consortium is composed of affiliated travel agencies whose purpose is to enhance the volume sales' profits of independently-owned travel agencies. This is done by means of group advertising, production of promotional material, educational opportunities, consulting resources, suppliers' discounts and other aids. This development has occurred to meet the challenge of mega-travel agencies which have a greater bargaining power with the suppliers. A recent example of this development is an arrangement arrived at between North-Western Airlines, Thomas Cook, a mega-travel agency, and Ford Motors whereby Ford personnel are expected to travel by North-Western through Thomas Cook only. North-Western in turn gives a better price to Ford travellers and a higher commission to Thomas Cook. The consortium concept seeks to achieve the same bargaining position for small travel agencies.

These concepts have also seeped down to other countries during the first decade of the new millennium.

In India, Thomas Cook has introduced their bid or buycom site which offers last minute bargain sales of international tickets as well as holidays—both domestic and international. Many products are on sale.

India Outbound

Outbound travellers from India touched four million mark during 2000—up from only 1.9 million in 1991. Till the mid eighties, Indians—particularly the leisure travellers—were discouraged to go abroad and foreign exchange was not released in their favour, if they declared their purpose as leisure. Foreign exchange was only released to travellers declaring their mission as business promotion, official or occasionally medical treatment abroad. The bureaucrats and politicians used the release of foreign exchange as patronage. At one time, Indian travellers could take only US$20 with them if they were on any mission other than business or official. How did they manage with this paltry sum in countries where even the taxi fare from airport to city costs more? Well, either they were sponsored by their friends or relatives abroad or they cheated—collecting US dollars from an intermediate point where they had parked their dollar accounts secretly, or buying it in black market paying more rupees. It was a peculiar philosophy of the Government to save foreign exchange. They encouraged their citizens to cheat. Overseas, Indian travellers were not respected as they acted like beggars. The scene changed a little when in the late seventies, the Government of India allowed US$300 for leisure travellers, later raised to US$500 in three years and some travel agents in India started marketing tours with this amount on shoe-string budgets. It became possible as air ticket could be bought in Indian rupees and for sightseeing purposes, buses and trains were used abroad which were relatively less expensive.

However, India decided to liberalise its economy in early 1990s. The country achieved an average growth rate of 4.5 per cent annually during this decade, with an accelerated growth in the later part of the decade. Allied to a strong economic growth, demand for international travel increased Until 1996, basic travel quota allowed by the Government—(BTQ) remained at US$500. It was increased to US$2000 per year per person in June 2000 and later, further enhanced to US$3000 a year. Now, it is US$5000 a year per person. For business travellers and for those attending conferences or those going for medical treatment, the foreign exchange quota was enhanced to US$25,000—up from US$15,000. The system was further simplified as the release of foreign exchange was administered by designated commercial banks, as a matter of routine and the people did not have to get prior clearance from the Reserve Bank of India or the

Government, for foreign exchange quota to travel overseas. It acted as a major stimulus for overseas travel.

ECONOMIC INTERNATIO NALISATION

The liberalisation of economy has resulted in greater exposure to the international business community and increased travel among the middle classes, who could afford to travel. There were other factors too—popularity of colour TV in India—with almost every other household having one or two colour TVs at their homes in urban areas. Indian films were shot in far-off foreign destinations like New Zealand, Switzerland and other European countries thereby twelve creating interest in these foreign destinations. The market is now big enough to attract twelve foreign government Tourist Boards to open representative offices in India, to lure Indian citizens to their respective destinations including Great Britain and Australia. The departures from India in the year 2000 were 3,996600—small for the size of a country like India but growing at a fast rate—specially in the leisure segment. The outbound travellers were 3.5 million in 1995 and 3.8 million in 1998. And, about 4 million in 2000.

Purpose of the Trip

Pure outbound leisure tourism in India is still in its infancy but it has grown out of all recognition compared with ten years ago and continuing to increase at a rate of fifteen to twenty per cent annually. According to an International Passenger Survey done on behalf of the Government of India in 1996 - 97, thirty per cent of the outbound tourists were travelling for business-related purposes, twenty per cent were visiting friends and relatives, thirteen per cent were joining their families, thirteen per cent went for employment and only thirteen per cent declared their purpose as pure leisure. India being a vast country, purpose also varies from region to region depending on the nature of the people. Most leisure travellers came from metro cities but the share of smaller towns was not insignificant. The impact of liberalisation of the economy is spread all over the country.

PATA report estimates that at present some twenty-five million Indians are affluent enough to be able to afford overseas holidays. With only four million Indians travelling abroad, the potential is six times more and it is rising with levels of incomes going up in the country.

Within the broad spectrum of outbound travel, the composition of the outbound market has changed radically in recent years. Business travel has changed from being a market composed primarily of businessmen and entrepreneurs pursuing business opportunities within the region, to encompass incentive and conference travel, as well as long-haul trips for increasing number of Indian companies with offices overseas on the one hand and multinational companies based in India on the other. Indian as well as multinational companies sponsor incentive travel holidays for their good workers or salesmen, or hold seminars and training programmes for their staff abroad. Travel Corporation of India (TCI), one of the largest travel outfits in India, reported sending eight thousand Indians in one year, representing white goods manufacturers—automobile and pharmaceutical sectors. Air India reported that such groups could vary from two hundred to UK, to five hundred to Singapore. American Express has estimated that business travel out of India is worth more than US$1 billion a year.

Survive

Only eight years ago, travel agency industry worldwide was in a state of euphoria as profits were soaring, business was up, commissions were high and airlines wooed the travel agents as their main source for higher sales. The number of travel agency outlets all over the world was increasing at a fast rate. Almost at the same time, an internet *Guru,* Dr Nicholas Nagarpente, predicted at the annual convention of PATA in Auckland, that three years from now people will be able to make direct bookings of all their travel plans by moving one finger on the mouse of their personal computers. Since then, the business of internet has increased at a fast pace leaving everyone amazed. Travel is an information-based industry, already exposed to computers for twenty years and the impact of internet on this business is most marked. A downhill trend in travel agency business worldwide is already evident. Many travel agents have taken advantage of the challenge posed by internet and started their own websites, reaching a much larger audience. ASTA conducted a research study of the member travel agents and discovered that sixty-seven per cent of their members were now charging fees for their services as commission income was not adequate, thus making up the loss due to capping of travel agency commissions. Again, the travel business worldwide has grown from an average of three to five per cent annually. According to the Travel Industry of America (TIA) survey, the business conducted on the Net in 1997 was US$900 million while the total travel business in the country was estimated to be US$500 billion. By 2002, TIA estimated the business on the Net will soar to US$9 billion but the overall travel business in the USA may well be nearer to 800 billion US$. The business on the Net will thus be only 1.2 per cent of the total travel business, leaving the rest to travel agency players—enough for everyone to have his share of the cake.

PARAMETERS OF INTERNET

In today's marketplace, it is necessary to talk about internet as a channel of distribution. It makes direct selling from suppliers to the consumers easy and hassle-free. The internet is an evolving communications tool with greater potential than any of its predecessors. Information technology is beneficial to every major principles like airlines, hotel chains who can market their products worldwide on their websites; the tour operators can market their destinations. National Tourist Organisations can have their websites to expose tourist attractions of their countries; individual travel agents can showcase their products—fair chance to all the players.

But it is only the travel agent who can add value and pleasure to the product. We were, therefore, not surprised to read a research paper which revealed that for every person ecstatic about booking on the Net, there were many more who were frustrated by the vast data and bewildering information which their head could not digest. Another IATA research further tells us that of the five passengers who book globally, four come through travel agents—not very different than what was happening thirty years ago. Again, only one in five explores the surf for information—but only one in ten actually books.

E-commerce is coming of age; in fact, it is doubling every three months. Creating this growth are supplier' websites and internet booking services such as Microsoft Expedia, Sabre's Travelocity, Internet Travel Network, Preview Travel, American Express and Travel Web, etc. These are full service mega sites doing business in millions. Most airlines too have mega sites but they only give their schedules and prices. They do not give comparative prices. This difficulty is overcome by sites like, www.travelocity.com, which gives comparative prices as well as airline schedules. There are several other websites offering similar services. Although the impact of internet on travel agency business is going to affect it adversely in the long run, the travel agent will not be out of business. European budget hotels are some of the best beneficiaries of the internet revolution— receiving bookings from all over the world from travellers wanting economical accommodation.

According to Cyrus Gazdar, former President of the Travel Agents Association of India and a leading expert on new technology, by 2005 the revenue of travel agents from travel agency commissions will come down by fifty per cent.

The Indian Scene

India is one country where IATA discipline still holds. Though the price war has left no standard tariffs—all airlines are offering major discounts to sell their seats including those with excellent reputation as dependable carriers. Another innovation in the Indian market is the emergence of consolidators, appointed by airlines to offer cut-throat prices. Consolidators are bulk-buyers of airlines seat who then retail it to individuals as well as travel agents, keeping a small margin for themselves. Another new institution to reappear in India will be travel agent Co-ops or Consortia as in USA. It may be in the offing as the industry reshapes.

The number of IATA-affiliated travel agencies in India has not declined, in fact it has increased from one thousand two hundred two years ago to about one thousand five hundred at present. Travel business in India is increasing at a good rate—five per cent annually. Outbound business is even better, the shortage of airlines seats make travel agents kind of indispensable.

Adi Katgara, Director TCI, expressed his anguish at airlines policy to introduce consolidators, throwing away their seats to beat each other in preference to regular IATA travel agents who worked for them for small commissions. Now, they end up paying higher commissions unprecedented in the history of Indian travel industry. Another development in Indian travel industry is the merger or amalgamation of large Indian travel outfits with much larger multinationals. The trend was started by Airfreight Ltd. with Carlson, followed by Sita Travels joining the Kuonis. This is an indication of the shape of things to come and we can predict more mergers, but it is good for the travel industry of India. Both our inbound and outbound tourism will grow.

Role in Domestic Tourism

TCI is also active in domestic tourism, though it is not their strongest area.

Specially designed for the Indian holiday market, the TCI's "24 Carat Indian Holidays" are flexible and economical packages to popular holiday destinations like Goa, Shimla, Kulu-Manali, Darjeeling, Bangalore, Mysore, Ooty, Kodaikanal, Kerala, Andaman Islands, Lakshadweep Islands, Mahabalipuram and Delhi-Agra-Jaipur.

During the four decades of its existence, TCI has grown from strength to strength mainly due to its creative marketing approach to tourism. In promoting international tourism to India, TCI has several firsts to its credit. It was the first Indian travel agency to open offices overseas. It responded to the needs of the market and wherever it found potential, it opened an office. For instance, it opened its office in Tokyo immediately after the Japanese started travelling overseas in the mid-sixties.

Now, it has opened an office in Beuros Aires to tap the tourist potential from South America.

TCI is also one of the first to introduce automation in its operations and put up its website: www.tcindia.com to market tourism services worldwide.

The success of any modern travel agency depends upon its ability to respond to the needs of customers—TCI seems to follow that golden rule.

7

ROLE OF EXHIBTIONS AND FAIRS IN TOURISM PROMOTION

Travel Industry fairs and exhibitions are the major marketing vehicles in today's highly competitive market place. In the rapidly changing world and with a view to keeping pace with new innovation in products, travel fairs and exhibitions have a special significance and importance. Today, no country, howsoever advanced and developed in technology, can afford to keep itself aloof from participating in travel fairs and exhibitions. These are considered an effective way to facilitate contacts, for exchange of information and ideas and to initiate sales in many industries.

In the present day world, no country can be self-sufficient in any field inspite of technological advancements. Rapid innovations in various fields make it difficult for any country to keep pace unless the knowledge and experience is shared together on a common platform. Almost all the countries in the world organise travel fairs and exhibitions of one kind or another in small, medium or a large scale. Several countries have put up permanent exhibition grounds, complexes equipped with state-of-art facilities to accommodate as many exhibitors as possible or just to participate. The scale of participation is constantly on the rise especially in well known travel fairs. Some times it is not possible for several exhibitors to get the space because of increase in the numbers of participating countries wanting to display their products. In several cases the space booking is to be done well in advance of the event dates.

Participating Advantages

International trade fairs and exhibitions give an opportunity to the exhibitors of participating countries to meet a large number of buyers and exhibitors from different countries at one place, to study the market trends and to compare the price and quality of similar products. In addition, participation in trade fairs open up avenues for locating new markets. The trade fairs and exhibitions also provide a common platform to participating countries to come together under one roof and exchange technical know how and personnel as well as help promote joint ventures between two countries. Apart from the presentation of exhibits, the fairs also provide a platform for exchange of knowledge and information through a medium of seminars, workshops, symposia on related exhibition, by experts from participating countries.

Participation in trade fairs also provide an opportunity to the exhibitors from participating countries to assess their own progress *vis-a-vis* that of the exhibitors from other countries and the steps necessary to achieve better performance and results. The importance of the fairs can also be assessed by the fact that they are organised not only by different trade bodies or chambers, but also by semi-government and government bodies which assist in organising such fairs send their official representatives to participate directly or indirectly. Following are the advantages to the exhibitors:

(a) transfer of technology and know-how between countries;

(b) exchange of information and technical know-how under one roof;

(c) assessing the progress *vis-a-vis* that of the other country and steps necessary to achieve better performance;

(d) creating better conditions for two-way communications among international partners in the market;

(e) creating proper surroundings or encounters and dialogues between suppliers and customers.

Certain important action areas, which are to be taken care of by the prospective participants in order to get maximum mileage from the fair, need particular mention. The following observations are considered to be of practical importance for those who are planning to participate in the trade fairs and exhibitions:

(a) Visitors to trade fairs are normally senior and high-ranking executives with decision-making power;

(b) Transaction of actual business may not come through and this should not disappoint the exhibitor. It is not unusual for some period of time to lapse before business deals are concluded. The participation in the fair should primarily be utilised to establish as many contacts as possible and to initiate discussion with prospective business partners;

(c) Systematic collection of data on visitors is very important as it will help in follow-up action. A business opportunity should not be missed on account of a delayed follow-up or due to failure to give the required information immediately on the spot;

(d) No opportunity should be missed to cultivate the media. Through this contact, the product will receive the required publicity;

(e) The importance of the type of publicity material prepared for the fair can hardly be overemphasised. This gives an opportunity to the visitors to go through the contents at his leisure;

(f) Use of audio-visual media with emphasis on the product will greatly help the visitor identify the product;

(g) The representation at the stand needs to be high level so that discussion with the visitors are meaningful. First impressions are extremely crucial and help a great deal in transacting the business;

(h) Opportunities to hold business discussion with the customers should not be missed. In addition to transacting business with existing clients, it is necessary to contact the new clients;

(i) Competing products should be examined with a view to updating one's own product. Trends in pricing, design, packaging, distribution, etc., should always be studied with a view to achieving better results in the competitive market; and

(j) Exhibition authorities bring out comprehensive catalogues of all the exhibitors. It is necessary that the exhibitor gives complete information to fair authorities about the firm and its products for inclusion in the catalogue. The catalogue is used quite often as a reference book even after the fair is over.

HISTORICAL BACKDROP

It was in the late 1950s that the first attempts were made to establish and organise fairs. The main objective of fairs for the tourist industry from the very beginning was two-fold:

1. As "public fairs" the purpose is to enable travel agents and tour operators, hoteliers, carriers and National Tourist Offices to establish contact with their markets, especially with the travelling public, and thus to promote their programmes and services.
2. As "trade fairs" in the more specific sense, their aim is to create opportunities for contact and business discussion, contract negotiations and exchange information within the industry itself.

In relation with the first of these two objectives, tourist fairs are often combined with exhibitions organised by manufacturers of sports equipments, both water and winter, camping and caravan equipments or by leisure industries. Since the emphasis here is on the consumer, the fair gives greater emphasis on their requirements. In many of these exhibitions there is a direct sale. On the trade side, the trade fairs are mostly for professionals and the emphasis here is on purely transacting business. During the trade fairs, conventions and annual assemblies of trade associations are sometimes held in conjunction with the fair. In major travel generating as well as receiving countries, the organisation of travel trade fairs has become a regular annual event.

The first such travel trade fair known as the International Tourism Borse (ITB) was held in the year 1967 in Berlin. Since then, there have been a number of other countries which organise travel trade fairs regularly. The enthusiastic participation in these travel trade fairs is a result of the ever - expanding travel trade

Travel Industry Fairs : A large number of exhibitors participate in these fairs representing all segments of travel industry and include travel agents, tour operators, hoteliers, airline companies, shipping companies, national tourist organisations, etc. In addition, travel trade media is also present.

Over the years there has been a steady growth in the number as well as participation in the travel trade fairs. Not only this, the organisers have been increasing the number of participants. New exhibition complexes are being constructed to give the travel trade fairs a modern look. The reason for the spurt in the travel trade fairs can be attributed to the involvement of tourism organisations in the marketing of tourism, particularly international tourism. It has been increasingly felt in the travel trade circles, especially those responsible for marketing, that the medium of travel trade fairs is a cost - effective way of communicating. Exhibitions by their very nature enjoy economies and advantages of lower costs because of the scale. The sheer size of the exhibition also makes it to be the great attraction, both for buyers and sellers of a tourist product.

Participation in travel trade fairs have several inherent advantages which are responsible for the growth in their numbers over the years as also the participation. Some of these advantages of participating in the travel trade fairs are as follows:

(a) Opportunity to both buyers and sellers of tourism services to meet under one roof and transact business;

(b) Lower cost of participation because of the advantage of scale;

(c) Effective vehicle of communication with clients;

(d) Better quality of attendance;

(e) Single platform to introduce the product (in the form of a brochure);

(f) Easy access to travel trade media;

(g) Cultivating new business contacts;

(h) Acquiring new information about the travel product;

(i) Opportunity to see the competitors' product; and

(j) Opportunity for effective public relations.

There has been an appreciable growth, both in the number of people looking for convenient places to display their products as well as consumers, to inspect and get an opportunity to buy these products. The travel trade fairs are the most convenient places for this to happen.

Every organisation which has to do something or other with tourism business feels it necessary to participate in these fairs either as an exhibitor or just a visitor. Participation in the travel trade fairs in fact has been a very important issue. The advantages of such a participation have been amply recognised. However, the question arises as to where to participate. Each travel firm would like to get maximum advantage with minimum cost from participation in a trade fair. Because of the multiplicity of events, making a choice has become rather difficult. Besides, there are various types of fairs available in different countries where participation is possible. There are the international fairs, both trade and consumer, the regional fairs and the national fairs.

Although international fairs like World Trade Mart (WTM), International Tourism Borse (ITB), International Tourism Exchange (ITE), International Brussels Trade Fair (BTF) are very popular with the travel trade, there are some other fairs also where participation is quite significant. The two most popular international trade fairs, however, are WTM in London and ITB in Berlin. Almost everybody who is somebody in the travel business likes to be seen in these two prestigious travel marts. Attendance as well as interest in these two fairs have been extremely high ever since these fairs have been organised.

UFTTAA Survey : Market Research Section of the Universal Federation of Travel Agents' Association (UFTAA) conducted surveys with the objective of determining as to who are the people who attend several of these fairs and what they hope to gain by participating. The UFTAA Survey was first used at the annual congress of UFTAA in Vienna and then at the International Brussels Trade Fair (BTF) in Brussels and the World Travel Market (WTM) in London. The sample of the survey consisted of over 100 participants at each of the above events. Each participant was asked 70 questions, of which 15 allowed an "open response". The major findings of the survey showed that travel industry trade fairs, though competitive, attract many of the same travel professionals and that an overwhelming percentage of those attending participated in the trade fair because they expected to gain business at each of these fairs.

Survey Report

The UFTAA Survey findings were published in 1986. The following were the main findings of the Survey:

(i) 80-95 per cent of participants at the above three events expected "positive practical benefits" from their attendance;

(ii) Three main motives for attending the trade fair were: forming of new business contacts, acquiring new information and promoting their own services;

(iii) About half the participants at both the fairs were travel agents or tour operators;

(iv) The suppliers of services like hotel companies and airlines were the next largest group;

(v) The average age of participants at BTF in Brussels was over 40 years in case of 70 per cent of the participants as compared to under 40 in case of 64 percent at WTM in London;

(vi) More than half of the participants at the two trade fairs were from outside the country where the fair was located (58% in the case of WTM). Most of the foreign visitors, however, were from receiving countries rather than from buying countries;

(vii) Advanced publicity for BTF was received largely through direct mailing (42%) and only through trade press (24%) and national associations (17%); on the other hand publicity on WTM was received largely through the trade press (49%) rather than direct mail (29%) or national associations (16%);

(viii) Regarding importance of press coverage for the event, 43 per cent of those interviewed at BTF said that the same was important as compared to 96 percent at WTM who believed that the fair was an important event;

(ix) ITB and WTM in that order are the most important trade fairs in the industry according to participants at both trade fairs;

(x) Comparative attendance at other trade fairs shows that many participants at WTM also go to ITB (43%), but few attend any other trade fairs (11% go to ASTA, but fewer attend all the others). Participants at BTF, on the other hand, participate extensively in other trade fairs;

(xi) The most stimulating themes for seminars and workshops according to the participants were topics on travel agents versus direct sale, automation, incentive travel, licence regulation, insurance issues, marketing, commissions, and sales through videotex.

Advantages : In addition to ceremonial and official events, the programme at trade fairs includes a series of seminars and workshops, discussion panels and presentations by private firms and official organisations including National Tourist Organisations active in tourism. The seminar programmes include half/full day sessions on important subjects such as International Conference and Conventions, marketing and promotion, modern information techniques, prospects and forecasts for international tourism.

Travel Trade fairs provide an opportunity to travel agents and tour operators of acquainting themselves with latest trends in the travel and tourism world under one roof with every sector of the industry represented, Each contact made during the fairs gives a certain return on the company's marketing investment to travel agents and tour operators. Trade fairs provide an efficient and cost effective international business environment where new products and services can be presented and negotiations on future contracts made.

Travel trade shows provide an opportunity to a tour operator to introduce his products in the form of a travel brochure and put the same in front of a buyer as travel show networking proves more valuable for individual operators because many buyers go to travel trade shows already holding established contracts with other sellers. Travel agents look forward to these shows to receive new products and negotiate future deals.

Worldwide, there are several travel industry fairs held at regular intervals which are frequented by the members of travel trade. These are held throughout the year. Some of them like ITB, WTM have however become quite popular with the trade and attract very large attendance as compared to others. In fact, these two events claim to be the largest, attracting a large number of both buyers and sellers from around the world and can be called international events of the travel industry.

International Tourism Borse (ITB) : The ITB as it is popularly known in the travel trade world was held for the first time in the year 1967. The ITB's story commenced way back in the sixties. In the year 1966-Messe Berlin provided space for nine exhibitors from the world of tourism at the Overseas Imports Fair and also staged a two-day convention in the Berlin Congress Hall. It was these two events that gave birth to the world's largest travel and tourism trade fair.

The publicity and the marketing of the fair by the organisers made it very popular in the subsequent years. In the year 1972 the fair attracted over 1,30,000 visitors from over 60 countries. The ITB organisers in the year 1973 included annual convention of the Active Members of the ASTA, the American Society of the Travel Agents. The ASTA subsequently held its 1975 full convention in Berlin coinciding with ITB of that year.

From its inception in the year 1967, ITB today claims to be the world's largest travel trade fair. In the year 1995, about 5,250 exhibitors representing 172 regions and countries of the world attended the fair. More than 52,000 trade visitors and over 60,000 private travellers transacted business. The trade visitors attending ITB '95 included 29 per cent from outside Germany.

Survey Findings : Based on a survey conducted by an independent trade fair market research institute and reported in Messe Berlin Press Release in March 1995,42 per cent of exhibitors were able to finalise deals at the ITB

1995. They reported signing contracts in the following sectors of the market: holiday and recreational travel (64%), business travel (32%), incentive travel (26%), educational and study trips (23%), conferences and congress travel (19%), sports travel (15%), adventure tours (13%), travel to health resorts and for health reasons (7%) and other contracts signed (18%). Based on their numerous contacts with the international tourism industry, 34 per cent expect follow-up business to be good, and further 48 per cent think it will be satisfactory.

Among the general public visiting the fair, 89 per cent intend to take at least one holiday and 70 per cent of them have already decided on their destination. Among those who have made their decision, more than half have already made their bookings. Altogether 81 per cent of general interest visitors stated that they would be booking a trip based on information and ideas obtained at the ITB '95.

One in four trade visitors (24%) was able to sign contracts during ITB '95. The sector in which the most business was conducted was that of holiday and recreational travel, with 52 per cent. Other contracts were signed in the following sectors: business travel (18%), adventure tours (14%), incentive travel (12%), educational and study trips (12%), conference and congress travel (11%), sports travel (9%), travel to health resorts and for health reasons (5%), and travel for other purposes (8%). Trade visitors signed contracts with exhibitors from the following countries/ regions: Germany (43%), European Union (26%), Central and Eastern Europe (18%), North America (18%), Central America/ Caribbean (15%), South America (14%), East Asia (14%), Africa (14%), Australia/New Zealand/ Oceania (10 per cent) and Western and Central Asia (8%).

Trade visitors in ITB '95 represented the following sectors of the tourism industry: travel agents (24%), tour operators (18%), carrier (15%), hotel companies (14%), institutes (11%), tourism offices and associations (8%) and national tourism organisations (7%). Twenty-nine per cent of the trade visitors attending the ITB'95 came from outside Germany, the majority of them from Austria, Poland, Italy, Switzerland, France, Spain, the United Kingdom, Belgium, Greece and Russia.

The International Tourism Exchange also includes a series of extensive supporting programmes. These include seminars and workshops, discussion panels, and presentations by private firms and official organisations including National Tourist Organisations active in tourism promotions. The seminar programmes include sessions on international conference and conventions, marketing and promotion, modern information techniques, prospects and forecasts for international tourism and a host of other important topics. Over the years the scope of the fair is being widened to incorporate more areas of interest in the field of tourism. For instance, the congress "Electronics in Tourism" has been introduced with a view to updating the travel trade in the latest technology concerning use of electronics in various tourist trade fields. ITB has also become an annual venue for several regional meetings of travel agents and hotel chains.

Originally being held for a period of seven days, it is now held for period of six days. During ITB '95 a Travel Visitor's day was devoted entirely to business contacts. No general public is allowed on the exclusive trade visitors' day. The travel fair is normally held in the month of March each year. The total available space for exhibitors is around 163,000 square metres.

World Travel Market (WTM) : Like ITB, World Travel Market is another, important event meant exclusively for travel and tourism professionals. Popularly known as WTM, The world Travel Market is an annual event held in London (England) every year in the month of November. WTM was first organised in the year 1980, as an international forum where the world's travel industry members meet to exchange ideas, establish new contacts, launch new products, and develop new business.

WTM attracts several thousand industry professionals every year from a number of countries. Similarly number of industry visitors is also increasing each year. According to organisers, WTM was attended by over 29,000 industry visitors in the year 1998 from over 138 countries. The industry visitors included tour operators, retail travel agents, hotel companies, inclusive organisers, group travel organisers, business travel agents and tourist transport companies. Almost 50 per cent of the total industry visitors, however, were tour operators and travel agents.

WTM has evolved a unique feature since the last few years whereby the exhibitors can meet the leading buyers with prior arranged appointments. This feature is the membership of the Meridian Club. Meridian Club is a business club for industry buyers open only to those buyers nominated by the exhibitors. Main stand holders (exhibitors) are entitled to nominate four buyers per square meter of contracted stand space. For example an exhibitor with 25 square meter stand can nominate 100 buyers. The companies which are sharing space with main exhibitors are each able to nominate 20 buyers. Meridian Club benefits to the exhibitors include an exclusive two Meridian Days during the Mart to meet only the industry's leading buyers, access to Meridian Club and pre-arranged appointments. The club membership gives a range of other advantages which include:

1. Pre-registration and advanced event information.
2. Advance exhibitor list to enable members to pre-arrange business appointments.
3. Express entry and a complimentary welcome business pack which includes event catalogue.

Meridian Club membership includes senior managers of the companies having decision - making powers to transact business deals on behalf to their companies.

World Travel Market has recently launched a new high-tech "database driven" web-site that delivers personalised information and various services designed to make participation more effective. The most interesting new feature is the "meeting scheduler" a tailor made appointment booking service which enables Meridian Club members to request meetings with main or space sharing exhibitors. Meridian Club members select who they wish to meet, view their available time slots and request a meeting. A summary e-mail is sent to each exhibitor each week detailing any new accepted or declined meetings. This new technology at WTM according to the organisers will help buyers and sellers to make the most of their time at World Travel Market.

World Travel Market provides an opportunity to the exhibitors to present their products and services and negotiate future business contracts. By providing a system of prearranged appointments with prospective new clients as well as existing ones, the forum provides an opportunity for generating additional sales. It also helps maintain high visibility among the international travel media.

International Brussels Travel Fair (BTF) : Popularly known as BTF the International Brussels Travel Fair is held every year in the month of November in the city of Brussels in Belgium. The city of Brussels has a unique advantage of being the capital of the European Community and its geographical location in the centre of Western Europe gives it an advantage over other cities in organising the travel trade fair, with increasing international participation. The three-day event is held between Thursday and Saturday. Started in the year 1975, the fair was being held in four halls having an exhibition space of 12,000 square metres (gross) and 8,000 square metres (net). Since the last two years that fair venue has been moved to Hysel exhibition complex with more exhibition space and modern facilities.

The BTF is more a technical than a promotional event. It may be described as a workshop. All the three days of the duration of the fair are for the professionals and they are, therefore, of great interest to operators, hoteliers and travel agents. The Brussels event is said to have proved consistently profitable for its organisers during its 25 years of operation.

Salon Mondial Du Tourism Et Voyages (SMTV) : Popularly known as SMTV, the Salon Mondial du Tourism et Voyages is held in Paris every year in the month of February. The fair is held for a period of six days of which the first two days are kept exclusively for the trade visitors. Travel mart is planned for subsequent days. Trade attendance at the mart is quite impressive. The fair organisers organise a buyer's and seller's mart during the trade days.

The SMTV had its first fair in Paris in the year 1975, in a spacious exhibition complex covering a gross area of 24,000 square metres (net 12,000 square metres). The venue of the fair has since been shifted to a most modern exhibition complex in La Defense, located at the west end of the city of Paris.

Feria International Tourismo (FITUR) : Spain has a special significance in the field of tourism. Few other countries in the world receive as many tourists as Spain in one year. The total tourist arrivals even outnumber the total population of the country. Spain also holds the key to the Spanish-speaking markets. Tourism being a major industry, the holding of a trade fair in the country was therefore considered to be crucial. Spain's international tourism fair (FITUR) was first started in the year 1980. The fair is organised each year in the month of January in a spacious exhibition complex of Madrid's 1,800 hectare Casa de Campo. The total exhibition area consists of about 15,000 square metres. The fair is held for a period of six days out of which the first three days are exclusively devoted to trade. The fair in Madrid places major emphasis on the Spanish speaking markets. This is because participation in the fair boosts tour programmes in Latin America as well as in Spain itself.

Travel Trade Workshop (TTW) : A travel trade fair on a smaller scale but with a stronger orientation towards the public in general is the Tourism Trade Fair 'Salon International Tourism' held regularly in early spring each year in Montreux, Switzerland.

The Swiss lakeside resort of Montreux provides an excellent picturesque setting for the first of the season's major travel events. The trade fair is held for a duration of three days in the month of 'October each year. The event is meant for professionals only.

Started in the year 1975, the Tourism Trade Fair is a leading event of its kind in Switzerland. Special trains and buses are utilised to bring in professionals from other parts of the country. The total exhibition space covers 10,200 square metres of the Montreux Congress Centre.

The exhibition stands include the official tourist offices of various countries, travel agencies and tour operators, regional tourist offices from different parts of Switzerland, companies promoting the sale of vacation homes like caravans, etc. A large portion of the exhibition surface is allocated to companies manufacturing camping equipment, photo and cinema equipment, mobile homes, pleasure boats and launches, etc.

European Incentive and Business Travel and Meetings (EIBTM): The Geneva meeting and incentives exhibition, known as the European Incentive and Business Travel and

Meetings Exhibition, is a buyer-seller meet in the area of incentive and business travel. The major objective of the EIBTM is to encourage the expansion and development of the incentive travel industry through a programme. Carefully selected international buyers travel to the event and stay free, a concept pioneered by EIBTM as a major initiative to guarantee attendance by leading buyers. Held for the first time in the year 1988 at Palexpo Exhibition Centre, Geneva, EIBTM is classed as 'World Ranking' event in the area of incentives and conferences. A new visitor promotion campaign for the exhibition includes:

(i) Increased target for hosting quality buyers;

(ii) New meeting and incentives consultancy service to offer free service to participating buyers-

(iii) Regular market bulletins to keep industry contacts uptodate with what buyers perceive to be business trends;

(iv) A computerised 'World Who's Who in Business Tourism' is prepared for the exclusive use of buyers which enables them to pinpoint key suppliers from over 100 countries.

The EIBTM is held every year for a period of three days in the month of May. The display area is over 12,500 square metres.

In addition to the major travel trade fairs, there are, however, some more important events drawing a good number of exhibitors and professional visitors. Some of these are as follows:

International Tourism Exchange (ITE) : Started in the year 1979, the fair is held every year in the month of February. It covers a gross area of 65,000 square metres. The fair is held in the Milan fair-grounds.

Swedish International Tourism and Travel Fair (TUR) : Started in the year 1982, the fair is held every year in the month of March in Gottenburg, Sweden. The gross area of the TUR is 20,000 square metres (14,200) square metres net. A separate area is set aside for camping.

Dutch Travel Trade Exhibition (TOUR) : Started in the year 1981, the fair is held every year in the month of December. It covers a gross area of 14,850 square metres. The fair is held in a spacious RAI Exhibition Centre in Amsterdam and is a very well organised fair.

Among the trade fairs discussed it is recognised by travel trade that only two, i.e., the ITB and WTM, are truly of international character. The global character of these two trade fairs can be judged by the fact that a large percentage of exhibitors as well as visitors are from overseas. Although organisers of most of the other fairs also claim these to be of international character, these are the only national exhibitions with the participation of some overseas clients.

In between the few international exhibitions and scores of national exhibitions, another interesting range of regional exhibitions have also surfaced. These regional exhibitions are normally organised by one or the other of the regional tourism organisations such as Pacific Asia Travel Association, etc. These associations specialise in setting up regional shows in prime target markets abroad.

Pata Travel Mart : Pata Travel Mart organised by Pacific Asia Travel Association needs special mention. The Travel Mart is geared to bring worldwide buyers of Pacific Asia Travel product services to meet with PATA member supplier organisations. The core of the Travel Mart concept is the appointments system whereby meetings are held during private scheduled business appointments. This enables buyers and sellers of Asia/Pacific travel products and services to meet in pre-scheduled, private business sessions to discuss and contract business for the coming years.

PATA makes efforts to secure the participation of tour wholesalers, conference and incentive planners, tour operators, corporate travel buyers and leading travel agents from around the world to meet with representatives from member hotels, airlines; cruise lines, government tourist offices, auto rental companies, ground operators and other suppliers. The names and business profiles of these participating buyers are furnished in an "Advance Guide to Buyers" and mailed to all registered booth contacts. The contacts are then requested to review the Appointment Guide and discuss with their staff the types of buyers they would like to meet during the Travel Mart. This information is then passed on to PATA via the Appointments Request Form. Buyers are also asked to review the Appointment Guide of Sellers and advise PATA of sellers' representatives with whom they would like to have appointments during the Mart. The information is put into a computer and schedules appointments are made for both contacts and buyers according to the following priority system:

1. Buyer and seller wish to meet each other.
2. Buyer wishes to meet seller.

Appointments are not scheduled based on requests by sellers only. An on site appointment scheduling session is held immediately prior to the start of the Mart to enable the sellers to book additional meetings during unscheduled periods of the Travel Mart schedules. Seller requests are provided to the buyers to inform them of the sellers' interest in seeing them during the Travel Mart.

After the computer scheduling has been completed, one receives a copy of his appointment schedule approximately two weeks prior to the Mart. Every buyer receives a copy of his organisation and forward copies to all his Travel Mart delegates. A secondary appointment schedule, reflecting cancellation that occurred subsequent to the appointment scheduling, are given to all delegates during registration at the Travel Mart site.

The participation in the Travel Mart is, however, limited. Among the buyers, the eligibility is restricted to only the delegates whose organisation has received an invitation to participate. The buyers are to be from organisations which are either doing business in the Asia/Pacific or have the ability to develop programmes and send their clients to PATA areas. Among the sellers, only delegates from PATA member organisations, that have registered as a booth-holder or co-exhibitor for the PATA Travel Mart, are eligible. The delegate category includes sales and marketing representatives of carriers, hotels, ground transport companies, auto rental companies, and destination promotion organisations.

The number of travel industry fairs have increased since the first travel trade fair known as the International Tourism Borse (ITB) was held in the year 1967 in Berlin. Many countries now regularly organise such fairs. This is a result of the ever expanding travel trade industry. More and more industry fairs are being added in the list of existing events. Earlier in the chapter some important established travel trade fairs have been discussed; some recent additions include the following :

1. International Tourism Trade Fair (ITTF) Zagreb, Croatia.
2. British Travel Trade Fair (BTTF), Birmingham, England.
3. Moscow International Travel and Tourism Exhibition (MITT) Moscow, Russian Federation.
4. International Travel Expo (ITE) Hong Kong.
5. International Tourism Asia, (ITA) Hong Kong.
6. Feira International de Lisboa (BTL) Lisbon, Portugal.

7. International Mediterranean Tourism' Market (IMTM) Tel Aviv, Israel.
8. Swedish International Travel and Tourism Trade Fair, (TUR), Gothenburg, Sweden.
9. International Travel Exhibition, Copenhagen, Denmark.
10. Arabian Travel Mart, (ATM) Dubai, UAE.
11. India International Tourism Expo and Mart (IITEM), New Delhi, India.

Participation in travel industry fairs is a costly affair for the exhibitors because of the rising cost of renting a space. In addition, to the high cost of stand, the exhibitor has to spend a considerable amount of money on decorating the stand, travel publicity material, receptions etc. Any exhibitor, therefore, has to take into account the relevant advantages which will be available to him *vis-a-vis* the cost of participating. In order to achieve maximum benefits from the participation, certain basic norms are to be taken into consideration with a view to achieving maximum mileage. These would include the status of the fair, whether it is of international or national status, expectations from each fair, in order to determine its value, type of competing exhibitors, quality and the attendance of buyers, timings of the fair, etc . Careful planning will go a long way in obtaining the best results from the participation in the travel trade fairs and exhibitions.

8

TOURISM PROMOTION BY AIDS

In today's changing and competitive international marketplace, advertising is important. Advertising is an activity designed to spread information with a view to promoting the sales of marketable goods and services. As such, it operates in two ways: first, by spreading information amongst consumers about the possibilities of consumption, and second, by seeking to influence their judgement in favour of the particular goods which are the subject of the advertisement. Any organization which uses this promotional instrument has to use certain media space which is paid for. In other words, we can also define advertisement as "paid public messages designed to describe or praise a product". This product in tourism is any destination area which is visited by a tourist. The media space for advertisement can be bought in newspapers, general and specialized magazines, in the form of posters or billboards. Besides the use of paid media space in the form of newspapers, magazines, etc., use of media time is also made in radio and television in order to transmit a pre-determined message to a predetermined audience.

Advertising has several inherent advantages in this method. The biggest advantage is its *wide coverage.* Advertising is especially appropriate for communication with a large number of prospective purchasers of a commodity or a service. A uniform sales message is directed towards all prospective purchasers. An advertisement can be placed before a large number of prospective customers as compared with the efforts of a salesman. *Frequency* is another advantage. It can make its appeal more frequently, whereas the calls of salesmen are usually not so frequent. Another advantage is its *accessibility.* It may reach prospects whom salesmen would find difficult to interview, owing to lack of interest, or inaccessibility to salesmen. Advertisement may reach such prospects through many types of media and under a variety of circumstances, and may thus attract their attention and arouse their interest. *Lower cost* is another major advantage. Large numbers can be reached economically, i.e. at a lower cost per contact than in any other technique available.

Advertising may be used to do a variety of selling tasks. A great deal of advertising attempts to win acceptance for the product. Such advertising may produce few specific demands for the advertised brands, yet when retailers display or show advertised goods they sell more readily than non-advertised ones. Therefore, retailers often hesitate to handle non-advertised goods unless they are obtainable at low prices. Advertising thus directly stimulates sales to retailers. Advertising may at times be used to make the complete sale. Some direct mail and periodical advertising attempts to make sales by requesting readers to forward orders accompanied by the necessary payment. When the number of potential buyers is small and when they are widely scattered, it could be extremely costly to reach them through salesmen. Advertising then becomes the most economical means of doing the entire sales job.

Planning the Advertising : While planning the advertising, the agency must give careful consideration to the actual make-up of the advertisement. This headline copy, illustrations, colour scheme, size, layout, and method of printing or reproducing the advertisement must be planned very carefully. This is necessary in order to gain attention of the customer, maintain his interest in the message, and secure the action desired by the seller. Closely related is the question of periodicity of advertisement. How frequently to advertise? For instance, is it better to use a full-page advertisement once a month or a quarter-page weekly? A frequently presented thought is likely to force itself into our consciousness. People are inclined to believe statements they hear or see repeatedly and hence the logic of frequent repetition of advertisements. In starting a special campaign the advertisements should not be spaced regularly. Early in the campaign they should be used close together, while later on they can be issued at much longer intervals. This is desirable because consumers forget rapidly; at first and much more slowly later on. After the facts are retained; by the prospects, the advertisements can be presented at much longer intervals.

Media Selection : The advertiser should give careful attention in planning to the selection of the medium or media especially adopted to his needs. The selection will depend upon the factors like the area to be covered, the type of audience to be reached, the appeals to be used and upon the services and facilities of the particular medium in relation to costs. The important factors which influence the media selection are: (i) media habits of the target audience; (ii) product characteristics (for example, TV may be the appropriate medium for those products which may require a demonstration of their operation for effective impact on the target audience); and (iii) cost of the media.

Message Selection : The message selected for use in the advertisement should be such that it retains the interest in the minds of the customers about the product. The customer must maintain his interest in the message, and secure the action desired by the seller of the product. The objective is to present the advertiser's message in such a way that the illustration may lead the reader to favourable considerations of the advertisement. The important characteristics of an effective message are:

Information: It should be adequate for a decision;

Interest: It should be able to catch the attention of the target audience;

Authenticity : It should avoid exaggerated claims;

Persuasion: It should be capable of creating a favourable conviction in the target audience; and

Memory Value: It should have something in it which can help the target audience to remember it.

Cost of Advertising : The agency must relate the estimated cost of the objectives planned and the contribution expected from advertising. Can the advertiser carry on a campaign large enough to make it effective? Are the funds available or will they become available through the sale of the product. How much the agency spends for the advertising? The various methods commonly used are:

Affordable Method: Here, the advertising budget is set on the basis of what the agency can afford;

Percentage of Sales Method: In this case, the agency sets the advertising budget on the basis of specific percentage of sales;

Competitive Parity Method : Here the company sets its budget to match those of its major competitors;

Objective and Task Method : In this the advertising budget represents the outlay required to perform the various tasks which are necessary to achieve the properly defined advertising objectives of the company. This method is considered the most rational.

Defining Advertising Effectiveness : In today's world, advertisement through any medium has become extremely expensive. Hence, it is important for the agency to ensure that the money spent on it does bring returns by way of increased sales. This could be done by way of evaluating or testing the effectiveness of advertising. Testing methods may be used to evaluate the results of an advertising campaign. By evaluating and analysing the effectiveness of advertisements that have been used, future advertisements may be improved. In addition, tests may be applied before advertisements are run. Pre-testing of an advertisement prevents expenditure that would not be profitable and leads to expenditures that give the best results. In determining advertising effectiveness the commonly used methods are given below.

Inquiries: Answer-back coupons, with same inducement, are incorporated in many advertisements. The amount of response is an indication of the effectiveness of the concerned advertisement.

Recall Tests: Here the respondents are shown the magazine cover or any other medium in which the concerned advertisement has appeared. They are then asked to tell which advertisements in that publication they remember.

Recognition Tests: Here the respondents are shown the advertisements and asked if they have read them.

Sales Tests: Here the actual sales results before and after the concerned advertising are examined. The sales results in the selected 'test markets' are also compared to those in some chosen 'control markets', i.e., the markets where the concerned advertising is not done. This is done to eliminate certain factors, other than advertising, which may also have influenced the sales.

In tourism, advertising is used extensively for promotion of various tourist products. This is a far cry from the era when colourful folders and posters were the only apparent form of travel promotion. In the field of tourism, advertising is mainly used to create initial awareness and interest in the tourist service or destination to be promoted and motivates potential tourists to decide to make further enquiries about costs, bookings, facilities, etc. It implies indirect communication with selected target groups—the potential tourists—through paid messages designed to praise a particular destination or an area. For a country which is trying to attract tourists, there can be two principal forms of advertising: (i) consumer advertising and (ii) trade advertising. To reach a wide number of consumers, such media as newspaper advertisements, radio spots, TV prime-time advertising are used. However, this form of advertisement is very expensive. For a developing nation it is extremely difficult to afford such a type of advertisement because of financial constraints. Trade advertising, on the other hand, is an indirect form of advertising and an economical method.

A large number of people today travel in groups. A tourist for various reasons chooses to travel as a member of a group, as opposed to travelling individually. The result, therefore, has been that a number of large tour operators have established their offices in such market areas. While the tour operator puts together inclusive tour packages, the tourist merely pays one package price for all services and is assured of a holiday. Such packages are then sold in retail by numerous smaller travel agents located in various market areas, and the result is that a group is formed. For a country which is trying to market its product, the area towards which these efforts are aimed is thus narrowed down to the important tour operators/ wholesalers. The media used to achieve this is large-scale advertising in travel trade journals and newspapers of international repute having travel sections.

Advertising plays a crucial role in marketing a tourist product. If the right combination of conditions is present the effect of advertising would be to increase the demand for the particular country's tourist product. Among the factors favourable to the successful use of advertising are the rising trend of demand in the particular product and an opportunity to stimulate selective demand, i.e., preference for the particular product. This is most likely where, there is a possibility of product differentials, and where consumer satisfaction depends largely on hidden qualities that cannot easily be judged at the time of purchase, or where strong emotional buying motive exists as in the case of tourism.

The American Marketing Association has defined advertising as "any paid form of non-personal presentation and promotion of ideas, goods or services by an identified sponsor". However, there have been several other definitions of advertising. One definition that may be accepted as related to all kinds of advertising is "the planned and controlled communication of persuasive ideas to a defined audience". The question may arise as to the selling function of advertising. The answer to this question is that while advertising will certainly be contributing towards sales, it cannot and does not always complete the sale.

A variety of other factors contribute to this and include pricing, distribution, dealer cooperation, etc., and all these jointly with advertising make up what is today called marketing activity. Mail order advertising, where readers send in written orders in response to press advertisements or home-delivered catalogues, is perhaps the single instance of directly related advertising selling. In other cases advertising acts as the communication factor contributing to the total selling function. In the case of service products such as tourism, banking and insurance, the direct selling action of advertising is rather limited. It must, however, be stressed that this does not mean that advertising is less important for such products.

Advertising Campaign : Any organization, in order to promote its product, has to resort to advertising to achieve desired results. Tourism organizations all over the world resort to this communication tool. Launching an advertising compaign for promoting a product is very crucial and has to be done in a planned manner. The term 'product' in the larger sense includes not only tangible products like furniture or a motorcar but also service products such as tourism, insurance, etc. There are various stages through which any advertising campaign must evolve.

Defining the Product : Before one can develop any communication of advertising for a product it is essential to know what it is that the product offers to consumers. This is very important. When you advertise soap, you are not advertising a cake of compound of alkali and oil in an attractive printed pack, but you may be advertising beauty or deodorant protection or youthfulness. To assess, therefore, what the product means to the prospective users we have to first ascertain the benefits that the users will derive from the product. Here are a few examples of this kind of benefit derivation:

- Car tyre can offer confidence, security or safety;
- Household cleaning can offer convenience, pride or hygienic conditions;
- Cosmetics can offer romance, self-confidence or glamour;
- Cigarettes can offer social status, confidence;
- Travel can offer rest, relaxation glamour, confidence or status.

The above examples show that in most cases the user benefit is not always apparent as a product feature. But it must be remembered that people buy things for the benefits they derive when using them. We must look at the product through the mind and eyes of the user. To do this it is sometimes necessary to conduct research amongst users or prospective users to find out what it is that they get from particular products. One can, at the same time, assess their knowledge, attitude and usage of competitive or substitute products so that the strengths and weaknesses of one's own product are known. This study of consumer assessment is important as in any system of communication the idea existing in the mind of the receiver will affect the interpretation of the message being received. In some cases it may prevent the message from either being noticed or perceived, let alone being received or understood.

Once we have arrived at this product benefit definition, we must then study this in relation to other factors. First, relative importance to the consumer of the several product benefits—the more important the benefit the greater its motivating values. Second, the relative position of one's own brand and substitute brands in regard to these product benefits—to create a unique and memorable message, the main ideas or benefits should be as distinctive and different from others as possible. Let us now assume that we have studied our product and its users and potential users attitude towards the product and have arrived at a definition of product benefits which we feel are most important.

Defining the Market Segments : We have a product. We know what users expect or want from it. Now we must assess how many users we have and where they are located. Most of this information will have been collected through various sources and supplied by the organization marketing the product. The kind of information that should be available will relate to the following:

Consumer Information

Type of Consumer : Number, sex, age, socio-economic profile;

Location of the Consumer: Whether they will be found in cities, small towns or rural areas or in all and in what proportion in each;

Geographic Distribution: Whether there are any regional variations in the market spread and if so, why;

Shopping Habits: The amount or size of individual purchases, the frequency or number of times a product is brought during a month or a year, whether bought on a regular planned basis or through an impulse decision ,at point of sale;

Decision Making: Often the person who actually buys the product does not always make the decision. It, therefore, becomes important to find out who it is that makes the decision and also the extent of the actual buyer's role in changing or influencing this decision. The reason for finding this out is to get an idea as to whom the advertising message should be directed. The person who decides is very important and in the case of joint decisions it may well be necessary to direct the advertising to two or more decision makers.

Distribution Information : Types of outlets, number of such outlets and the importance of each type; the location of these outlets in different cities, towns and rural markets; the dealer's part in the selling activity.

Sales Information : The trends over the years and any significant shifts that may have occurred in different geographic areas and the reasons for these changes is very important information. Seasonal variations that may be related to weather, festivals and other local and national reasons are also very important. In giving us all this information the manufacturer will not merely be giving us information about his product but also of competitive and substitute product against which his product will compete. All this information will provide us with a knowledge of the dimension of the market so that we will be in a position to assess which particular markets are of greater importance. This will also assist in creating the media plan to reach each market and also in creating relevant messages for each. In terms of media selection, the statistical information that will be supplied will enable to plan a campaign using media which will provide cover, reach and frequency related to the market definition.

Attitude Segmentation : This relates to segmenting the market by user motivation. For example, it has been shown that certain types of people use certain products in larger quantities and more regularly than others. In the same way, some people travel more often than others. These groups are termed the heavy-user group. And, in most cases, it is not the usual socio-economic categorisation that distinguishes them. This may be termed as attitude segmentation or separation. The problem in such segmenting or separating into two groups is that unlike socio-economic segmentation it is difficult to physically isolate the group. This can, however, be achieved through segmenting as it were the advertising message. It is important to note, however, that this sort of segmentation should not be overdone. Social appeals or segmented campaigns should only be developed if it is found that there are large enough groups of consumers who have attitude which would respond to such appeals. Often, however, it is not only the advertising that is segmented but the product itself is separately produced for each of the segments. At this stage we will have progressed from product definition to a knowledge of the market, its size, location and, different segmentation patterns.

Interpreting the Marketing Objectives

What we have been discussing until now is information of the environment in which the advertising campaign will have to work. As we know, since advertising is only the communication aspect of the total marketing function we have to take into account the marketing plans of the both enterprises in the long-term and short-term, and relate the advertising to these. The marketing objectives that are given by the enterprise will detail the plans that the enterprise has for its product in the coming year and in some cases for a few years ahead. These plans would cover items such as:

(i) The sales targets for the coming years broken down into regional targets or others, as the case may be.

(ii) The distribution, merchandising and sales promotion activities planned to support the sales increase;

(iii) The role that advertising is expected to play in creating consumers;

(iv) The inhibiting factors which will work to prevent the enterprises from achieving the target, competitive products and their advertising, consumer attitudes, etc.

It is important to note that in any marketing operation the product formulation, packaging and pricing, distribution and availability at point of sale are all of vital importance. All that advertising can do is to bring consumer to the point of sale. But if the product is not properly made, packaged or priced or is not well merchandised or promoted at point of sale and, therefore, is not visible, then it is quite possible that the sales effect of the advertising will not fructify. This brings out the importance of integrating these various activities.

Once we have got clearly the marketing objectives of the enterprise and their plans in relation to these objectives, we can see what advertising has to communicate and to whom with a view to provide the maximum relevant support to the agreed marketing plan.

Planning the Advertising Campaign

We now know what we have to sell, to whom we have to sell, where the prospective consumers are located and also how the product will be made available to them. Our object now is to create an advertising campaign which will reach target audience and motivate them to come to ask for and buy the product. We have now processed all the facts that the enterprise has given and have perhaps had a dialogue with the consumer, through research, to ascertain his knowledge, attitude and usage of the product and its competitors. As a result, we have found out the proposition that we feel would be most motivating. We have also found out where the consumer is located, how and when he buys the product. We are now in a position to get down to work on two aspects which make up an advertising plan. These aspects are: (i) the creative strategy and (ii) the media plan

Creative Strategy: Creativity in advertising is very crucial as on this depends the comprehension of the customer to understand the product. We now have to transform proposition or statement into an idea which is to be communicated to the customer. In converting the proposition into an idea, use of creativity is of paramount importance. Creativity must take into consideration direction and relevance. For the bright idea to be useful, there must be a right idea. It is this idea which has to be communicated to target group. In order to communicate the idea, media personnel, production personnel as well as creative personnel will have to be involved in this area. Finally the idea will have to be channelised into various material that will be required for advertising campaign. This can range from press advertisements to film commercials, to radio spots and TV spots, to posters and other point-of-sale material. All these items will be creative interpretation of the idea.

The Media Plan: While creativity is perhaps most closely related in an agency with the development of an idea and its interpretation into advertising material, it also plays a role in the development of a media plan. Let us know briefly the way in which an agency constructs a media plan. Media may be defined as vehicles of mass communication which are used to carry advertising messages. Very rarely, except in the case of direct-mail advertising, are media developed solely as advertising communication vehicles.

One may broadly classify media into two groups:

(a) Media which are read, seen or heard by the consumer for their 'editorial' worth. These are the newspapers, magazines, the radio programmes cinema shows, TV programmes which are read or tuned into or watched by the consumer for the 'editorial' material which they offer. The advertising benefits from the editorial climate of this media.

(b) Media, usually more 'reminder' type of media such as outdoor media, hoarding, transportation signs, posters, kiosks, neon signs, etc., which are noticed in passing only. They obtain consumer exposure due to the fact that the consumer's living habits cause him to pass by them. For instance, commuters in trains and buses, motorists and pedestrians on roads are all exposed to such media.

The above group also includes point-of-sale items. In preparing media plans one has to study the behaviour and exposure of consumer groups with regard to both kinds of media. We have to study both kinds of media. We have to study what media our target consumer looks at for 'editorial' pleasure and when he does so and in what frame of mind. By studying consumers living habits and pattern of movement we can assess which of the second group of media he will be exposed to as a general rule. In the more advanced countries it is possible to get detailed statistics on the kind of audience that each medium has. In advanced countries this information is very detailed indeed and permits one to prepare accurate media plans. In other countries, however, this information is still very scanty and apart from basic circulation information it is rare that one gets much else. However, through experience one gradually builds up a fund of knowledge which enables one to select appropriate media for appropriate markets. Here, apart from the circulation information a study of the quality of the medium in terms of editorial content and style is a very useful method of evaluating reader types.

9

CLASSIFICATION OF ADVERTISING FOR TOURISM PROMOTION

Advertising can be classified according to various criteria. The major classifications are as follows.

CLASSIFICATION BASED ON FUNCTION

Advertising can perform 5 major functions, as follows :-

(a) It can inform the prospective customers about a product, service or idea.

(b) It can persuade the prospective customers to buy such products, services and idea.

(c) It can remove cognitive dissonance from the minds of the customers to reinforce the feeling that they have bought the best product, service or idea.

(d) It can remind existing customers about the presence of the product, service or idea so that the customers come to the firm or its distribution channels time and again to buy the same.

(e) It can dissuade customers or public at large from buying certain products or services that are harmful for the society or humanity.

Accordingly, there are 5 types of advertising, if we keep function as the decisive criterion.

Informative : This type of advertising informs the customers about the products, services or ideas of the firm or organisation. Examples: An introductory advertisement of a travel agency in a travel magazine. An introductory offer of *Tawa* Fresh *Atta* (wheat Hour) in newspaper (offering 1 *kg* of sugar free with every 5-kg pack to the residents of Delhi).

Persuasive : This type of advertising persuades or motivates the prospective buyers to take quick actions to buy the products or services of the firm. Examples: Free cash card scheme of Airtel. Titan's advertisement of 5 to *50 per cent* off on various brands of watches. Declaration of the last date for admission to a business school.

Anti-cognitive : This type of advertising reinforces the fact in the minds of the customers (who have purchased the products or services of the firm) that their purchase decisions were correct. It also informs them that the firm is ready to give all types of after-sales support to them. Examples: Advertisements giving details of after-sales service centres of a firm advertisements of engineering firms in the journals related to their trade; advertisements informing about the number of copies of a book sold.

Reminder : This genre of advertising reminds the existing customers to become medium or heavy users of the products or services of the firm that have been purchased by the them at least once. This type of advertising exercise helps in keeping the brand name and uses of the products in the minds of the existing customers. Even during the periods of depression, the sales figures of those firms have not been adversely affected that advertise, though they may resort to such measures only on a sporadic basis. During the times of depression, the focus is on reducing the losses; all the firms shall incur losses but advertising lends its helping hand in minimising the same. Examples: Exchange offers for old products with new ones (of same brands) on mixers, cooking ranges (e.g., Sunflame), pressure cookers (e.g. *Purane Cooker ke Badle Naya)*, televisions (Sansui exchange offer) and cars (Maruti).

Negative : This type of advertising dissuades targeted audience from purchasing such products and services as would harm them in particular and the society in general. Examples: Advertisements of various civic authorities against alcohol, tobacco and narcotics. Advertisement of the National Aids Control Organisation (NACO) persuading people not to indulge in free sex, lest they should contract the deadly AIDS disease.

Business-to-Business Advertising

This is done by the industrial manufacturer or his distributor and is so designed that it increases the demand of industrial products or services manufactured by the manufacturer. It is directed towards the industrial customer. The marketer chooses only trade-specific magazines or journals that the targeted customers are likely to read. The collective name of these trade-specific magazines or journals is Trade Press. Note that the buyers of industrial products are purchase managers, purchase executives, purchasers, project managers, large corporations, MNCs and government departments. In India, DGS&D is a major buyer of various types of goods and services. The Indian armed forces buy goods and services worth billions every year. Examples: Siemens, Larsen and Toubro, General Electric Co, Kirloskar Brothers. Limited and Gates India Private Limited.

Trade Promotion to Distribution Channel's Hook Members : This is done by the manufacturer to persuade wholesalers and retailers to sell his goods. Different media are chosen by each manufacturer according to his product type, nature of distribution channel and resources at his command. So, it is designed for those wholesalers and retailers who can promote and sell the product of the manufacturer. Such advertisements also inform about the taxation structure, terms of sale, appointment of new dealers, changes in prices, various schemes (for ultimate customers as well as for distribution channels) and above all, vital information about products and services so that these distribution channels could inform the ultimate customers through word-of-mouth promotional efforts.

Professional Promotion to Influence Professionals : This is executed by manufacturers and distributors to influence the professionals of a particular trade or business stream. These professionals recommend or prescribe the products of these manufacturers to the ultimate buyer. Manufacturers of these products try to reach these professionals under well-prepared programmes. Doctors, engineers, purchase professionals, civil contractors and architects are the prime targets of such manufacturers. These professionals, in turn, recommend these products to the ultimate buyers. Their recommendations are deemed final in most of the cases. Example: A doctor prescribes a medicine that is taken as the ultimate elixir to cure a disease and the patient does not question the doctor in this context. This doctor is convinced by medical representatives of pharmaceutical firms like Pfizer and Biological Evans. Examples: SKF, Birla White Cement, L&T and ACC cement.

Financial Promotion of 'Financial Tools : Banks, financial institutions and corporate firms issue advertisements to collect funds from markets. They publish prospectuses' and application forms and place them at those points where the prospective investors can easily spot them. Such advertisements ought to have legal approvals and the Registrar of Public Issues gives them the permission to undertake such exercises. Knowledge of national capital markets, stock exchanges, global stock indices, rules of the government in relation to share issues and guidelines of the SEBI is essential. The advertising agency hired by the firm in this context cannot bypass the rules of advertisement of these issues. It is mandatory for the advertising agency to declare the dates of opening an issue, details of over subscription of the issue and finally, the last date of closure of the issue in the media. The prospectus and form of the issue in question are also salesmen of the firm that goes public. It is advisable to get these designed from a professional advertising agency or get them printed at a reputed press.

Region based Division

We can also classify advertising according to region. We can have 4 types according to this criterion, as follows:

Global Promoting Around the World : It is executed by a firm in its global market niches. Reputed global magazines like *Time, Far Eastern Economic Review, Span, Fortune, Popular Science, Popular Electronics* and others are used for issuing glossy multicoloured advertisements. Cable 'TV channels are also used to advertise the products through them. Supermodels and movie stars are used to promote high-end products **Examples:** Intel (CPUs; through TV advertisements), Panasonic (stereo component systems; through magazine advertisements), Nikon (SLR cameras; through newspaper advertisements) and Omega (watches; through Cindy Crawford in magazine advertisements).

National Promotion in only one Nation : It is executed by a firm at the national level. It is done to increase the demand of its products and services throughout the country. Examples: Nirma *(Doodh* Si *Safedi Nirma Se Aaye).* Surf Excel *(Naya Surf Excel Hai Na).* Raymond *(The complete Man).* Whirlpool Refrigerator *(Fast Forward Ice Simple).* Galileo's advertisement in *TV Talk* giving it's the name of its web site www.galileoindia.com. Amadeus' advertisement in *Trav Talk Global Reach... The World at Your Fingertips... With Us, You'll Go Further... www.amadeus.co.in).*

Regional Promotion only in a Region : If the manufacturer confines his advertising to a single region of the country, then its promotional exercise is called Regional Advertising. This can be done by the manufacturer, wholesaler or retailer of the firm. Examples: Advertisements of NFL urea in regional newspapers (covering those states or districts where these newspapers are circulated), Orange cellular phone service (in Mumbai), Hutch cellular phone service (in Delhi) and Airtel cellular phone service (in Delhi).

Local Promotion in a Small City or Limited Area : When advertising is done in one area or city, then it is called Local Advertising. Some professionals also call it Retail Advertising. It is done by the retailer and his advertising plan is in line with the national-level or regional advertising done by the company he represents. The retailer can advertise to persuade the customer come to his store and buy. He may also advertise so that the customer comes to his store regularly and not for any particular brand. Examples: Su-kam Inverters (leaflet advertisements in a Delhi colony). Advertisement of Kaff Kitchen Products (newspaper advertisements in southern Delhi colonies or clusters only).

Targated Markets based Division : Depending upon the types of people who would receive the messages of advertisements, we can classify advertising into four sub-categories.

Consumer Product Advertising : This is done to impress the ultimate consumer. A consumer is a person who buys the product or service for his personal use. This type of advertising is done by the manufacturer or dealer of the product or service. Examples: Advertisements of Pepsi Cola, Van Heusen shirts, Peter England shirts, Elle 18 lipsticks etc.

Desired Response based Division

Two types of advertising emerge under this classification.

Direct Action : Promotion of Product Directly : This is done to get immediate responses from customers. Examples: Snowhite's Summer Sale, Purchase coupons in a magazine, Big Jo's Sale, Inalsa Maxie (Exchange Offer), Coca Cola (Free Coke with every ticket to Appu Ghar), The IA-Taj offer. Leaflets in a newspaper with purchase coupons printed on them, Wings of Freedom from the IA, advertisements of clearance sales on hoarding and cloth banners and TV commercials, asking the consumer to buy before a due date to avail hefty discounts.

Indirect Action : Indirect Promotion of Product : This type of advertising exercise is carried out so that it makes a positive effect on mind of the reader or viewer. So, he develops a favourable image of the brand in his mind. He would buy only that product or service whose image is positive in his mind. Examples: Advertisement of Delhi Traffic Police on TV.

Company Demand based Division

There are two types of demand, as follows :-

Market Demand: It is the total volume that would be bought by a defined customer group in a defined geographical area in a defined time period in a defined marketing environment under a defined marketing programme.

Company Demand: It is the share of the company in the market demand.

Accordingly, there are 2 types of advertising, as follows :—

Primary Demand Promotion for Increasing Primary Demand : It is also called Generic Advertising. This is category of advertising is designed to increase the primary demand. This is done by trade associations or groups in the industry. Primary advertising is done by many companies at the same time. But there is no competition. The idea is to generate an incessant demand for the product. The name of the firm is advertised but the objective of the exercise is to increase the demand of products of a particular class and not the demand of the products of that company. The broader interests of the industry are taken care of without laying much emphasis on the products of the firm that executes this type of advertising campaign. Examples: Advertisements for promoting diamonds (De Beers: *Diamonds are forever)* coffee, milk, eggs (NECC : *Sunday Ho Ya Monday, Roz Kahao Andey)* and other poultry products. Advertisements of insurance companies (e.g, LIC). Promotional advertisements of banks. Advertisements of manufacturers' associations of various types.

Selective Demand Promotion to Increase Company Demand : This is done by a company or dealer to increase the company demand. The company would advertise its own brand only. The retailer can also advertise a particular brand. Examples: HMT watches, Hero cycles, Philips stereo systems, Honda portable generators and Enchante jewelry.

Media for Advertisement based Division

There are 7 categories in this broad classification, as follows :-

Audio Promotion

It is done over radio and PA systems and through auto-rickshaw promotions, four-wheeler promotions etc.

Visual Promotion through Visual Displays : It is done through PoP displays, catalogues (without text), leaflets (without text), cloth banners, brochures (without text), electronic hoardings, simple hoardings, running hoardings etc.

Audio-visual Promotion through TV, Cinema : It is done through cinema slides, movies, video clips, TV advertisements, cable TV advertisements and campaigns on CCTV systems.

Written Display : It is done through letters, fax messages, ieaflets (with text), brochures (with text) articles and documents, space marketing features (in newspapers) etc.

Internet Promotion through Websites : The world wide web is used extensively to promote products and services of all genres. Read *Effective Business Communication* by A Kumar in this context. Various web sites of individuals and firms are, in fact, messengers of these firms that have been telling people from thew skies to buy their products, services and thoughts.

Verbal Promotion through Voice Gestures : Verbal tools are used to advertise thoughts, products and services during conferences, seminars and group discussion sessions.

Aims of Advertising : The following objectives of advertising have become relevant in the context of operations of the business and non-business firms in the new millennium:-

The Information

- To introduce new products in old markets.
- To introduce old products in new (or foreign) markets.
- To introduce new versions of old products.
- To give vital facts and data related to health, family planning, inoculation campaigns, elections etc.
- To combat competition in an effective manner.
- To convert light users into medium users and medium users into heavy users.
- To increase sales during off-seasons.
- To effect sales during peak seasons.

Cognitive Dissonance

- To reduce or eliminate cognitive dissonance from the minds of the customers who have Purchased the products and services of the firm.
- To remind the customers that their purchase decisions were the best ones.
- To sell more to the same set of customers by making them "feel good" after reducing their post-purchase cognitive dissonance.

- To obtain dealers' support.
- To build a positive business image in the minds of the public at large.
- To secure leads for sales people.
- To increase the number of units purchased.
- To maintain brand loyalty among the existing set of customers.

Brand Image

- To create a brand image through corporate advertisements.
- To sustain brand image through advertisements in print and audio-visual media.
- Society Oriented Image
- To inform the society that vital community issues are being -addressed.
- To give support to issues related to ecology and environment.
- To create awareness among the masses about issues like environment protection, pollution control, health and education.

THE ADVERTISEMENT

Advertising and Advertisement : The following differences have emerged after many research efforts of management thinkers Advertising is a process under which, we prepare a message and send it to the prospective or actual customer. But an advertisement is the message itself.

The advertising process takes place when the company gives funds to an advertisement ad agency. But an advertisement is not concerned with this feature of the process. It is designed to create a good response from customer. The objectives of non-commercial advertisements may be very pious and sans commercial overtones.

Advertising is a regular event but an advertisement is a complete unit in itself.

The advertising process generates advertisements of various types. But an advertisement does not affect the process of advertising.

Advertising and Personal Selling

The following differences are worth consideration :—

Advertising is effective and its cost is low. But the cost of personal selling is very high.

Advertising motivates the prospective buyer to purchase goods through non-personal methods. But personal selling requires the salesman to call on the customer personally.

Advertising can cover large areas or market niches. But personal selling can be done in a limited area.

An advertisement can be changed depending upon the market needs. But this is not possible in the case of personal selling; a salesman cannot change his attitudes, behaviour and selling techniques overnight.

Advertising cannot get an immediate response from the customer. However, an efficient salesman can collect orders with the power of his charisma.

Tourism World and Role of Advertising : Advertising is an integral part of our social and economic systems. It is a powerful technique of sales promotion and has been doing wonders in the domain of distribution because it is quite capable of influencing the consumption patterns of customers. It also affects the processes of production and distribution. That is why, it is said that advertising is the Archimedian lever that motivates the world of commerce and industry.

In this volume, we are chiefly concerned with advertising efforts of the tourism industry. The role of advertising in the tourism world can be analysed with 5 distinct players of its gamut, namely, manufacturers; middlemen, sales force, consumers and the society.

Advertising and Producers : Producers make the goods with a clear intention of selling them to earn profits. They are also keen to deliver satisfaction to the consumers (so that they could come again). They do take full advantage of advertising as a major weapon to popularise their products or services. Producers are prepared to spend a lot on advertising because it pays to do so. But in tourism industry, they do not take front- seats so far as advertising campaigns are concerned. Instead, they support wholesalers and retailers of the tourist industry in this process. They also build their images in the minds of customers by issuing image-building advertisements in the media. But they rarely try to sell their products and services to the ultimate customers. That is because they are not located close to their targeted markets but wholesalers and retailers have access to those markets. Example: A hotel located at Hawaii cannot sell its services to a customer located at Moscow. But a travel agency or tour operator having its office in Moscow can do the job for that hotel. In any case, the customer would trust the travel agency or tour operator in question because he can interact with its officials. Even if the hotel can be contacted by E-mail or telephone, the tour operator or travel agency would be able to get the best deal for that customer.

Advertising helps producers get 3 benefits, as follows:—

It Increases and Stabilises the Sales Turnover: The product or service manufactured by the producer may be the best but cannot be sold on its own. The information about the products or services should reach those who are interested in buying such them. In a highly sensitive and competitive marketing environment, profits of the firm can be maximised not by reducing the costs but by multiplying the sales turnover rate. Sales of the producer firm cannot be multiplied by advertising that involves additional expenditure. An image-building exercise would suffice in the cases of hotels, airlines, tourist resorts, theme parks, wildlife sanctuaries etc. .An effective advertising programme of the producer helps the customer form an opinion in his mind about the producer. The retail and wholesale channels do the killing on behalf of the producer. However, some hotels have also started advertising rates of their rooms or day/night packages in magazines and newspapers. The AI-Taj Holiday offer is one such example that shows a deviation from the trend described earlier. There is no harm in undertaking such campaigns if the producer can justify these expenses. But a tourist would go to a travel agency to get hotel bookings because he is keen to buy a complete package and not a small chunk of products and services provided by a particular producer. Quick turnover would mean less tied up capital, costs, wastage and losses as the stocks of on -the shelf goods/ services are held for shorter periods. Producers cannot help attain quick turnovers without the help of marketing intermediaries who are in regular touch with clients. Under normal business conditions, advertising helps not only in maintaining, but also in extending the sales turnover. During the periods of depression, the efforts of the firm's advertising department must not be brought to a naught. During such periods (e.g, lean seasons), reduction in losses is the major priority for all the producers. They may stop advertising. But they should not because happy times would come again (during peak seasons). Then, the customers would prefer them because these lean-period advertisements would remain in their subconscious minds.

It Maintains the Existing Market and Explores New Ones: A forward looking producer always has its eyes on the future business prospects, though it cannot afford to lose sight of the current financial position. A company's success is reflected not only in creating a market niche, but also in the maintenance and expansion of that very niche. New market niches may also be explored and won with the help of travel agencies and tour operators. When the force of an advertising campaign decreases in terms of frequency and coverage, the natural assumption is that the business of that firm is falling, or the products are not up to the expectations of consumers. A low ad-spend could also mean that the competitors are better in serving the needs of market niches. Out of sight; out of mind! This maxim is aptly applicable to the advertising game. It is significant to bear in mind that one of he functions of advertising is to help retain the present market. The other function is to create new market niches and divert the demand patterns for the further expansion of the existing market niches. Modern business situations warrant a forceful entry into new markets. In such newly explored markets, advertising does the spadework and creates a fertile ground for the sponsor (producer) to sow the seeds of prosperity for itself. The sponsor can get increased share in the new market through creative advertising. It may also culminate into its leadership in the new market.

It Controls Product Prices: Through well-designed advertising campaigns, it is possible to control the product prices, particularly retail prices. Very often, greedy retailers exploit the needy consumes by charging higher prices. If this consumer exploitation is not bridled, both the producer and consumer suffer for no fault of theirs. The manufacturer can help himself as well as his consumers by printing the retail prices on the product packages. Today, the package of the product is not only protecting the contents of it, but also it is serving as a powerful promotional tool. That is why, each product package states the price in lucid terms. It is usual to come across the statements on product packages like "Retail price not to exceed Rs..., Local Taxes Extra" or "Price and Date of Packing on Cap or Bottom." Such pieces of information save the skin of the manufacturer and help him get support of consumers. That is how manufacturers safeguard the economic interests of consumers. Advertising makes it possible for manufacturers and marketers kill two birds with one stone.

Advertising and Wholesalers : In the chain of distribution, tour operators act as the essential links between producers and consumers. Their existence is justified by the functions they perform and the services they render to both the producers and consumers. Advertising comes to their rescue in 2 ways, as follows:-

It Helps Them Build a Brand Image: IA tour operator has to create an image in the market that would draw travel agencies towards its fold. Naturally, he has to use the brand images of all those products and services that he buys (from many producers) on a bulk-purchase basis. Eventually, he has to sell these products and services under his own brand name. The travel agency must have a positive opinion about the tour operator so that it could sell its products and services to the ultimate buyer. Thus, advertisements of tour operators are normally image -building exercises.

It Supports Travel Agents Who do Real Selling jobs: And quite naturally, the tour operators also stand to gain due to these efforts. Travel agencies get their names and addresses printed or advertised in the advertisements issued by tour operators. These travel agencies are approached by ultimate clients. The travel agencies get in touch with their respective tour operators and satisfy the specific needs of these customers through alterations and modifications in tour programmes. The travel agents remain at the forefront in the advertisements issued by tour operators. They coordinate with producers most of the times and get their bookings for hotels, motels, resorts, bars, disco clubs, theme parks and other places in which, tourists are interested. Thus, they undertake back-end marketing exercises, which normally involve the purchase of various types of products and services from producers. Travel agents undertake front-end marketing exercises, which normally involve sales of various types of products and services to actual customers.

ADVERTISING AND RETAILERS

Retailers "(travel "agencies) use advertising to their advantage through the following 3 methods :—

It Guarantees Quick Sales for Them: Every retailer holding the stock of different producers, takes pride not in warming the shelves of his office but in quick and healthy turnovers. A travel agency does not have products or services in its offices but it is supposed to achieve targets set forth for it by the tour operator. Advertising, by bringing the wide range of these products to the notice of the consumers, quickens the pace of sales for travel agencies. More sales lead to reduced capital investments for tour operators. The profit of tour operators automatically leads to that of travel agencies. Example: A travel agency helps the tour operator sell the maximum number of air tickets, which were reserved by the latter. Thus, the tour operator, airline and travel agency stand to gain. Further, losses due to holding of stocks (hotel rooms, airline seats etc.) over longer periods are reduced, if travel agencies undertake advertising efforts in their respective market niches. Note that tour operators cannot undertake such types of campaigns. Thus, increased profits accrue due to increase of sales. Further, advertising gives much leeway to travel agencies to serve the needs of their regular and new consumers. Advertising gives golden opportunities to travel agencies during peak seasons.

It Acts as a Salesman: What a travelling salesman does for his organisation is done by a professional advertising campaign at least costs. That is why, most of retail organisations do not employ a large number of travelling salesmen; instead, they are willing to spend on advertising, which attracts consumers to their offices. In such offices, the counter salesmen or executives of the travel agency cater to the needs of these customers. In the new millennium, advertising has heralded an era of boom for those retailers who have been spared the problems of hiring, training, paying and controlling the travelling salesmen. Tour packages are sold to customers through E-mail, fax transmissions, telephonic conversations etc. Old customers only send the cheques and the travel agency does the needful. And how that is made possible? Simple! Advertising creates favourable impressions and images of the firm and its products of the minds of these (old and new) customers. But we must admit that salesmen may be told to cover the cities in which, they are stationed to book orders of corporate customers. In such cases, they are supported by the advertising campaigns of their firms. Such campaigns remind and persuade old customers and inform and motivate prospective customers. Salesmen do the killing jobs once they arrive at the offices or homes of such clients. They may have to give hefty discounts for selling tour packages.

It Helps in Maintenance of Retail Prices: Consumers are keen to get good-quality products at stable prices over a period of time. Each consumer has his own family budget where he strives hard to match his expenditure to his disposable income for maintaining a socially acceptable and accent living standard. If prices go on changing abruptly, these individual budgets are likely to be distorted to such an extent that the consumers may be forced to think of substitutes for the products they are using. Budget blues may involve a shift in brand preference. The advertised package tours publish the prices of products and services that are likely to be effective at least for 3 to 6 *weeks*. Consumers heave a sigh of relief as prices are more stable over a period.

Salesmen Get Support: The sales wing of a travel agency gets the support of advertising blitzkrieg. Direct efforts of the sales army and indirect efforts of advertisements help the travel agency clinch orders. Both are important and complimentary to each other. We must not undermine one at the cost of the other. The success lies in perfect dovetailing of these two efforts to satisfy the requirements of the travel agency. The top brass of a travel agency ought to get the best out of these two earners. The sales force gets the following benefits from advertising. Firstly, a good salesman is nothing less than an actor who, by his skill and mastery over the art of selling, tries to win the hearts of consumers for selling the products of his company. Sales acumen and skills have a value, esteem and the glamour only when he has a matching backdrop like a full-fledged advertising campaign. He may be active, tactful and versatile but the extent of his success rests heavily on the colourful background created by advertising. Salesmanship alone is like a song without music. Advertising persuades customers to come to him; then, he can prevail upon them to sell his tour packages to them. His song is likely to be more meaningful and result oriented if he uses his selling skills after advertising in the local or regional market niches. Secondly, it lightens his burden. A good advertisement reduces his selling effort; the customer already knows the details of the tour package and all he has to do is to discuss the basic *modus operandi* (for tour execution) with the salesman. In case, the salesman alone is called upon to accept the challenge of selling, it becomes much difficult to effect sales. In the absence of advertising during peak seasons, he is forced to play a double role-the role of an advertiser and that of a salesman.

Advertising provokes public interest, wins the confidence of customers and promotes conviction. With such tasks already done, the salesman is at ease to tap the opportunity through his personal acumen and efforts. That is why, a professor of advertising has said that selling and advertising are so closely knit that they may deemed a cup and a saucer, essentially made for each other. Advertising sells between the calls, the work of salesman is rendered easier. During the actual sales calls, he signs the deals with finesse. Thirdly, advertising instills self-confidence and initiative in the sales force. The victory of a selling organisation is, orchestrated by the psyche of its sales force rather than its number. A sales force that is self-confident and go-getter can get vital support from advertising campaigns from of the firm. Advertising instills self-confidence and initiative in the sales staff. The sales force is more determined, daring and aggressive as it handles the delicate jobs of convincing the customers.

Advertising and Consumers : The ultimate aim of all the marketing efforts is to satisfy the needs of consumers by transferring the benefits of productive efficiency (of the firm) to final users. Advertising is an essential concomitant of modern marketing mechanisms. It helps consumes in at least 3 ways, as follows:-

It Acts as a Driving force in the Decision Making Process: Advertising, through its variant forms and formats, disseminates useful sets of information about the relative merits and special features of the products and services in terms of prices, quality, utility, quantity, durability, convenience, time period of execution etc. It guides tourists to go ahead for a particular tour package, hotel, resort or fun park. The role of advertising cannot be underestimated in the process of intelligent or selective buying, if we have the gargantuan field of tourism in full view. Mr,. V Fenogenov said "Advertising helps find his way through the ever greater mass of products put out by the industry." The present-day complex world of industry has been able to provide the largest possible varieties of products to such an extent that consumers are at sea to decide. Further, each producer claims that his product is far superior to others. Example: Take a simple example of tour packages. In the newspaper, we would find many offers. But which one the customer should opt for? Which one is the best? Is it one by the SOTC or the one by the TCI ? Advertising comes to the rescue of the consumer. He compares the prices of similar tour packages and then, selects the best one out of these (according to his precise needs). Thus, the process of decision making is easier and quick.

It Ensures Better Quality Products at Reasonable Prices: Advertising stimulates the sales of a good product and accelerates the destruction of a bad product by imprinting the image of the product on the minds of consumers. It earns long-lasting reputation for the travel agency. Such an image can be created through effective branding strategies. Every brand stands for typical values of quality, value, guarantee, price and service". Brands display the net worth of a given product. Example: The label on each sachet or strip of a medicine gives its formula, side effects, dosage, frequency of use and price, including the dates of manufacturing and expiry. Maintenance of quality and price of a product is an important objective of any efficient firm. Moreover, improvement in the quality of the product and reduction in the prices by cutting costs, This approach goes a long way in making the product to move from local to national and international markets.

It Saves Time: The norms of modern living have made the members of any family put forth their best to eke out a living. In the past, products and services were cheaper and requirements of the family were limited to such an extent that a single breadwinner was enough to manage the show. Today, craze for modern amenities and luxury goods has changed the ambition sets of people. They are money-making machines, longing for more materialistic assets, luxury goods, luxury cruises and luncheons in five-star hotels. Everyone is racing against time to earn more money because its is deemed the most important commodity in the world. It can buy everything except peace of mind, though. These cogs in machines eagerly await the arrival of Sundays when they can have a day of total rest. For such people, advertising is a great time saver. They do not have the time to call a travel agency over telephone because of their busy schedules. They know about the products and services of different producers and wholesalers because they are extensive travelers. So, they read advertisements of retailers and get bookings done for tours and excursions. They use brand names to their advantage. Many of them have friends and/or business associates in reputed travel agencies. They call them over telephone and get their bookings done.

Alternatively, they tell their office staff to do the needful. Just like they visit a store and pick the goods, they contact the travel agent and get the bookings done for themselves or for their families. Money is not a constraint for these people who normally belong to the creamy layer of the society. They save valuable time; which otherwise would have been lost in locating, identifying and deciding about the tour package. Thus, they do not indulge in bargains. Finally, people from lower middle income strata of the society are also keen to travel through out the length and breadth of India. Many of them also go abroad, though such excursions are undertaken by them rarely (once every

3 *years).* These middle-of-the road families also use advertising to get the best deals. They indulge in bargains and even get some discounts.

Advertising and Society : Advertising is not only a business activity, but also it is a social institution as it affects every one in the society due to its sweeping sway and mesmerising powers. Every one in the society is benefited by this magical world of advertising. We can consider 4 specific benefits in this context, as follows :-

Uplifts Living Standards: Experiences of advanced nations have proved that advertising leads to improvement in the living standards of teeming millions. That is why, Winston Churchill once said, " Advertising nourishes the consuming power of man. It creates wants for better standards of living... It spurs individual exertion and greater production." The standard of living of a society is conditioned by its national income and its distribution on one hand and the consumption pattern and disposable income on the other. Generation of national income is deeply influenced by the value of advertising expenditure. That is because effective and faithful advertising gives stimuli to consumers. These consumers demand such products as are being advertised on radio, TV, cable TV, newspapers, glossy magazines, leaflets, brochures, catalogues etc. This effect, in turn, rotates the .wheels of production to produce not only more, but also better and cheaper products while keeping eye on quality standards. Improvement the standard of living implies high-volume, better and cheaper production, thus allowing more people of lower income brackets to enjoy such products as were hitherto beyond their reach.

Generates Gainful Employment Opportunities: Advertising is capable of generating gainful employment opportunities, both directly and indirectly, for those who have talent and courage. Direct employment opportunities are available in the branches of this ever-growing field. It is a highly specialised and challenging profession that requires the services of experts, artists, creative directors, copywriters, photographers, web masters, painters, content writers, singers, musicians, accounts executives and many more. It is a team effort. Professionals ought to be formed to handle meticulous and delicate tasks of the advertising process. Advertising campaigns are especially strenuous. Further, Today's advertising industry is banking heavily on supplies of paper, paints, colours, dyes and chemicals, stationery items, print production techniques, advanced scanning systems, DTP, electric and electronic gadgets and equipment, sound devices and visual aids.

Serves the Society: Advertising, though used as a technique of popularising the products or services of a firm, is a great educator. As a conveyor of socially relevant message, it has been utilised by different sections of the society, especially the NGOs and governments, to disseminate ideas, opinions and thoughts of great importance. Examples: Campaigns of anti-Polio inoculation. Protective measures described for driving vehicles. Use of the CAS through a set-top box in cable TV networks. News of demises and ceremonies related thereto (normally these messages are printed in newspapers free of cost).

Serves the Economic Interests of Firms and Prospective Employers: An employer fills the vacancies in his firm, an unemployed applies for a job, parents hunt brides and bridegrooms, film producers promote their films and cinema houses remind of regular and special shows. All these activities cannot be undertaken by them without the use of a mass promotion tool. Customers of their products and services are spread in vast geographical areas. Moreover, their whims and fancies cannot be gauged so easily by marketers. Thus, advertising is used to motivate those prospective customers who would be keen to buy their products and services. The hit rate is always low in the case of activities of a mass promotion tool. But it is worth the efforts in most of the cases. That is because revenues generated by sales to a limited number of customers are able to recover costs of advertising and other methods of promotion.

Entertains Children, Adults and the Youth: Each meaningful advertisement is a unique piece of information because each advertising copy has a definite theme behind it. In order to convey the theme of advertising to the markets, the sponsor tells a story, gives a statistical profile, narrates the history and describes the future of his product. Whether the readers or viewers of advertisements .act on these advertisements or not, they are benefited. That is because they are informed about a new style of delivery of a message. Advertising enlightens the general public in a delightful manner. Thus, it is a entertainer and educator too.

Depicts the Culture of a Nation or Develops a New Trend: Culture stands for the values of life and living that are ever changing as they are guided by the dynamics of social, political and ethical dimensions. There are two concepts to be discussed in this context. Firstly, cultural impact of advertising is quite obvious because the latter reflects the status quo of the former. The advertisements of the DAVP present the nation as one entity, despite her caste, class and communal diversities. We find a change in the values of life when the we see skirts of the past going above the ankles and then, just above the knees! What would happen next can be left to readers' imagination! So, who made mini skirts a fashion statement of the new millennium? Ad world, of course! The "cultural mirror function" of advertising reflects the present value system of the society. Advertising within the limits set by culture is to create new expectations for consumers. The world is 'moving' on the lever of advertising ('flying' should be the right word in this context). With the educative value, provoking force and invoking tinge, it affects thoughts, gestures and behaviours of those people who are its targets.

Consumers' attitudes, habits, likes, dislikes, fashion preferences and actions in every walk of life are deeply influenced by advertising. Secondly, the mad men of advertising are also responsible for imparting new values to the society. The producers of the new era create new products and services. Many of these may not be needed by the society. But these producers approach ad firms and tell them to produce state-of-the-art advertisements that would make these products or services instant hits. Thus, advertising can trigger new trends in the commercial and industrial markets of the society. Many firms cross the boundaries of nations and create such trends across the globe. Example: Intel Pentium CPO (P-4).

Physical Distribution

This is the fourth P of the tourism marketing mix. According to Kotler, "Marketing channels can be viewed as sets of interdependent organisations involved in the process of making a product or service available for use or consumption."

In conventional marketing exercises, products or services are delivered by producers to consumers through clearly defined distribution channels. The consumers of these product and services collect these goods from the last distribution points of these chains. The distribution channel of any marketing activity overcomes the time, place and possession gaps that separate goods and services from those that would use them. The members of distribution networks perform the following basic functions :-

Information: They collect information about customers, competitors, sales trends and other players of the marketing environment.

Promotion: They communicate the messages of marketers to customers through well- defined promotion campaigns and thus, help the marketers sell more products and services to those customers who pay them visits.

Negotiation: They strike deals on prices, delivery, ownership, transport and other vital aspects of distribution.

Ordering: They give orders to the manufacturers of products and services so that the latter could supply them these goods and services in time.

Financing: They provide funds for temporary acquisition and storage of goods or products that provide services. Distributors and wholesalers normally indulge in financing activities.

Risk Taking: They bear risk of carrying inventory and selling it to the next nodes of distribution channels.

Storage: They keep goods in their godowns so that the same could be distributed according to the needs of the customers of such goods.

Payment: They make payments to producers when goods have been sold. Normally, credit periods of *30, 60, 90* and *120 days* are involved; different industries have different credit periods.

Title: They take title of goods that are transferred to them for the purpose of pushing them to the next stage of distribution. Note that Kotler has defined the term Marketing Channels. These are different from physical distribution channels.

Sale of Product or Service based Division

We can either sell the product or we can sell a good image of OUI: company through advertising. So, we have 2 classifications in this context.

Product : Promot on Product : This is done to increase the sale of a product. It can be done by manufacturers of consumer or industrial products. It can be done for a particular brand as well.

Examples: Sansui's offers in newspaper advertisements. Pringle *(Special Privilege Offer).*

Service : Promotion of Service : Firms that give services indulge in this type of advertising efforts. Their objective is to attract customers towards their services.

Example: Airtel *(Free incoming calls to cellular phones).* Advertisements of travel agencies of various tour packages.

Concept : Promotion of Concept : The firm tries to communicate to the targeted audience that the concept would help them achieve better standards of living. Or, they would get better results as a result of acceptance of the concept promoted by the firm. But the insinuations are totally commercial in nature.

Example: Advertisements of small business houses, persuading targeted readers to surf through the Net and earn money. In fact, these firms would also earn money when these Net surfers would work for them.

10

PROMOTIONAL ACTIVITIES IN TOURISM

In tourism, sales support is all those promotional activities designed to transmit to the public and to the travel trade specific and detailed information on aspects like accommodation, transport, attractions, prices, etc., concerning the tourist services to be promoted. Sales support activities are the measures which establish personal or indirect contact with customers or trade intermediaries. It is also a process of training employees to be proficient salespersons. Sales support has certain distinct, closely related functions which neither advertising nor public relations can be expected to fulfil as effectively. It is a channel of communications between the 'manufacturer' or the 'producer' of a tourist service—accommodation unit, transport company, etc., and the 'distributor' or the 'seller' of that service. Secondly, it aids and assists the seller to do his job more effectively with the support of different techniques. The aim of the sales support activities is:

(a) to inform the customers (tourists—both actual and potential) or trade intermediaries travel agents, tour operators, airlines, etc. about the various services available, their price and quality, etc.;

(b) to assist them in selling these services to the ultimate users;

(c) to motivate them to devote a sufficient level of sales activity to the service promoted.

Sales Support Activities : National and regional tourist organizations as well as tourist service enterprises and tour operators recognise fully well that their sales and profit depend to a very large extent on the support and assistance they provide to retail travel agents and also the way in which they motivate travel agents. This is done by way of sales support activities. In order to be able to sell a service (a room in a hotel, seat in an airline) or a destination to the prospective tourists, travel agents or other sales intermediaries need to be aware of certain factual information which includes:

(i) Country's tourist facilities such as existing as well as new establishments, accommodation capacities, price schedules for various services.

(ii) Various travel regulations and formalities such as visa requirements, foreign exchange rules, health and vaccination regulations including different certificates needed, custom rules, rates of exchange for currency, etc.

(iii) The various transport and communication services available; the schedules of airlines, railways, road transport services, shipping services (where available), their rates.

(iv) Weather conditions at different times of the year, and types of clothing required during different seasons.

(v) The utilization (occupancy rates) of existing tourist facilities at different times of the year.

(vi) Plans for opening of new destinations, hotels, transport routes (railways, airlines, etc.) and also plans for expansion of existing tourist facilities.

Advertising has now created a demand in the form of enquiries made by potential tourists, travel agents and other intermediaries. The potential tourists, travel agents and other intermediaries would now require, in addition to the type of information mentioned above, materials such as brochures, folders, booklets, guide books, directories, maps and illustrations in order to be able to transform demand into definite bookings. Most of the above material is meant for distribution to potential tourists by the travel agents and other sales intermediaries like tour operators, airlines, etc., either directly or through mail. Almost all the tourist organizations and tourist service enterprises produce the material extensively and make use of it by way of distributing it to travel agents, tour operators, etc. Tourist sales intermediaries on their own also produce sales support material for distribution to potential tourists.

Sales Support Techniques : Sales support techniques can be grouped into two main areas— printed material and special offers. Printed material includes brochures, folders, direct-mail material, display material, etc.

Brochure is a pamplet bound in the form of a booklet. It is a voluminous publication with special emphasis on the quality of paper, the reproduction of illustrations, graphic design of the cover and the layout of the pages. Special emphasis is laid on the quality of the paper and printing. It is mainly used by official travel organizations and tourist service enterprises to inform prospective tourists about the attractions and facilities available in the country. A brochure describes and illustrates a destination or service in more detail. Detailed information on accommodation, prices, travel schedules, etc., is given in a brochure. Travel agents and tour operators use brochures as one of their principal selling aids.

Folder, on the other hand, is a single piece of illustrated paper which can be folded. Folder is less voluminous than the brochure and its production is less time consuming. These are usually printed on a single sheet and then folded. It is perhaps the most widely used advertising media by the official tourist organizations and by tourist service enterprises. It can be used alone or in conjunction with a sales letter. It is relatively inexpensive to produce and can be used in a variety of ways. While producing, special care should be taken about the quality of the paper and printing. Folder, compared to brochure, is short, tastefully illustrated and attractively designed and produced.

Sales letter is a direct-mail material. It is a tool through which an attempt is made to gain agreement or favourable action towards a product. Sales letters offer many opportunities for selling travel services. These could be used alone or in combination with travel brochures or folders. These are sent out to those people whose addresses have been selected according to the likelihood of their being potential users of the services offered. A proper mailing list is a prerequisite for effective use of this tool. Sales letters require very little time to prepare and to distribute. The effectiveness of a sales letter can be measured very rapidly from the response it draws. This is done by way of a reply card which is included with which the recipient can request further information and also travel literature.

Display material includes posters, dispensers for sales literature, cardboard stands, articles of handicrafts, exhibits, etc. This material is used in the agency's office or in travel agent's sales rooms. The material is displayed in such a way that it attracts the attention of a visitor as soon as he enters the office. In many cases, cinema slides are also used, either fixed or on an automatic projector for display purposes.

Special offers like temporary price reductions, free gifts, premiums and various types of contests are being used extensively in competitive industries like cosmetics, packaged foodstuffs, etc. The tourist industry has also started to adopt these techniques as an additional sales support tool. Reduced airfares for students, 'affinity group', special off-season rates at hotels and tourist resorts are the examples of some of the special offers in the tourist industry.

Public Relations Role

Public relations is an important promotional technique. It involves measures designed to improve the image of a service, to create a more favourable climate for its advertising and sales support activities. It covers such a wide range of activities and is used for so many different aims that it is not easy to define it. Public relations is the "art and science of planning and implementing communication and understanding between a company and the many different groups with which it is concerned in the course of its operation." Public relations may also be defined as the "continuous and consistent representation of an organization's policies to the public at large and to sections of the public who have a special interest in the organization's activities, e.g., to various strata of employees, shareholders, actual and potential customers as well as its local and national government. A positive attitude to public relations in an organization's activities is evidenced that it recognises a duty to keep the public aware of those activities, and of their impact upon society and its environments. From the definitions of public relations, it is evident that its main function is to inform public about the activities of an organization. In ether words it is a part of a firm's or an organization's total communication effort. Its purpose is to create best possible reputation for the firm or the organization by way of presenting facts. In a climate of favourable public opinion, an organization's or a firm's goals can be achieved more effectively.

In the field of travel and tourism, the need for making information and facts available to both potential and actual tourists assumes special significance.. It involves measures designed to create and improve the image of the tourist product, create a more favourable climate for its advertising and sales support activities, especially in regard to travel trade intermediaries and news media. Favourable acceptance of any tourist destination by the public is of utmost importance. In fact, no business is more concerned with human relations than the business of tourism. Public relations in tourism is used to create and maintain a positive image for a country, a tourist destination in the minds of people who are in a position to influence public opinion (journalists, editors, travel writers, etc.), or in the minds of sales intermediaries (travel agents, tour operators, etc.). It is oriented towards creating and maintaining an atmosphere whereby travelling public at large is convinced of the advantages of visiting the country concerned.

Public relations is one of the important functions of the official tourist organization. In fact, tourist organizations primarily are public relations organizations. The objectives of public relations in the field of tourism may be divided in two parts: the dissemination of information and the creation of a favourable image for the tourist product.

Public Relation Techniques : Public relations consists of a number of inter-related activities oriented towards creating and maintaining a favourable positive image for the tourist product. The main techniques of public relations in the tourist promotion are as follows:

(i) Organizing familiarization tours for travel writers, editors, travel agents, photographers and other key personnel from different parts of the world as guests to visit the country and to get first-hand knowledge about it. These persons then write about the country visited in well-known travel and other general interest magazines.

(ii) Organizing television and radio contests featuring the destination country.

(iii) Organizing press releases and arranging press conferences with key personnel connected with tourism field with a view to disseminate information about the destination.

(iv) Arranging seminars and workshops in the place where the tourist promotion office is located.

(v) Organizing cultural programmes, musical and folk shows, TV interviews, exhibitions and national friendship weeks in the country where the national tourist office is located.

(vi) Organizing various types of contests about the country.

(vii) Encouraging large departmental stores, organizers of fashion shows and manufacturing companies to project the country or a part of it as a promotion showcase in their premises. Public relation activities thus range from distributing a simple press release to newspapers to organizing familiarization visits for key personnel in the travel trade. It is used to create a favourable climate for sales support and advertising by transmitting facts and information to advertising media and to sales intermediaries. However, to have any prospect of success, public relations planning and organization should be an integral part of an organization's management strategy and must be organized on a continuing basis. Public relations function of an organization cannot be considered as an end in itself or as something which can be introduced at short notice to cope with a crisis situation. An organization should have a positive and planned public relations policy. It is no coincidence that most of the national tourist organizations devote considerable effort to their public relations programme.

Publicity for Tourists

In order to round off the total marketing effort, there is need for a well-planned publicity programme. Publicity refers to the dissemination of information without charge for its news value in order to inform the prospect about a particular product. A publicity programme could include regular publicity stories and photographs to newspapers, travel editors, contact with magazines on stories, ideas, and the preparation of story outlines and pictures in order to induce magazines to do feature stories on a particular destination. News releases to travel trade magazines on items of interest to the travel industry, such as opening up of a new area, total expansion, increased transportation facilities, development of a new resort are measures which are adapted together with other publicity through the media of radio, television, lectures, seminars, travel films, etc. Tourist publicity in the beginning developed in an empirical way under the pressure of the growth of international travel, and to the extent that information had to be supplied to an ever-increasing number of tourists. Thus, at its outset, it was simply informational publicity. With the growth in volume of commercial tourist publicity, particularly in the sphere of transport, and great increase in the number of tourists, various countries realized the importance of tourism in the national life. They recognised it especially in economic terms—earning of foreign exchange. This necessitated the countries to organize their institutional tourist publicity with a new approach and employ experienced commercial publicity technicians to draw up a long-term publicity strategy.

For a successful tourist publicity, one important factor is to be placed at the top of all considerations. In the field of tourism, motive forces and effects lie on different planes. The motive forces of tourism lie mainly on a plane which is outside the scope of economic factors, while the results of tourism are represented in a series of economic processes. Generally speaking, when reference is made to tourism, thoughts go to economic effects of travel and sojourn and an estimate is made of the value of tourism for the national economy in terms of the figures represented by earnings and the influence on the balance of payment of a country. The earnings of foreign exchange become very important. Reference is also made in tourism to supply and demand as market terms and the tourist plant of a country is evaluated according to the place it occupies among the national resources and its potentialities to increase the national income. This purely economic consideration accounts for the striving of every tourist country to obtain the most optimum possible share of the market and tourist publicity is a means of pursuing this effort.

DIFFERENT TECHNIQUES

The methods of tourist publicity in their evolution have lagged behind in comparison with the developments of the publicity methods of other branches of economy which utilize applied psychology and sociology. They are still mainly based on experience, instinct, routine and technique. Publicity still proceeds from the object with a more or less arbitrary combination of rational and emotional appeals and perhaps in consideration of the results obtained by research in publicity media, but in utter disregard of the person to whom the publicity is addressed. So it is not yet clear at all how tourism, whose fluctuating character was proverbial, has now grown into a phenomenon almost impervious to crises, or why the tourist need has undergone a re-classification to other needs in order of importance, as also why, despite the fundamental universality of the tourist need, different human groups have different conceptions about its composition and the urge for experience.

Professor Krapf was the first to undertake a close examination of the tourist consumption. It is of particular importance for tourist publicity when he states that all considerations of tourism must now free themselves from objective facts and institutions and cover the emotional world of man and the conduct of his life. This should be followed up by an examination of tourist behaviour. For the extension and importance assumed by tourism in a particular country or region, the decisive factors are neither the beautiful landscape as a natural assumption, nor the past and contemporary culture of a country, nor the natural medical cures in a region nor the transport and tourist plant in its costs and efficiency relationship, nor the appreciation of the authorities concerned or the favourable measures they may sanction. The determining factors are to be sought elsewhere, as in fashion, opinion, need, interest, which in their turn are to be appealed to as the irrational factors of tourist behaviour. The first named factors constitute the prerequisites of tourism which are publicised; the latter ones can be influenced only with the help of publicity. Considered in market terms, supply in the tourist sector is constantly expanding, its publicity efforts always increasing and getting more intensive and the media it utilises ever more diversified and multifarious.

Coordination of Measures : Rising demand and expanding supply characterise the present-day situation of the travel market with its publicity competition. In this competition, two methods stand out which are quite suitably designated as the methods of the advanced tourist countries and those of the developing tourist countries. The advanced tourist countries show a constantly increasing tendency towards a graded publicity beginning with the publicity of the individual travel trade firms, of resorts, areas, provinces and finally countries, while the developing tourist countries, begin with the country's publicity to which regional and travel trade publicity is added. As yet the differentiation between tourist institutions is too limited for them to enter into competition with each other. However, in the well-known tourist countries this competition takes place inside the country and finally between corresponding tourist resorts and enterprises. This carries in itself the danger of a frittering away of the forces and since the percentage of the ineffective residual part of local publicity is relatively large, it is necessary to undertake campaigns in a manner which is more than proportionate. This has special relevance to publicity abroad, where the desire for the most extensive possible coverage of the demand is somewhat restricted by the available financial means. This reason alone points to the necessity of concentration and coordination of all tourist publicity measures.

Brand Concepts : Each country is a travel mosaic composed of a variety of distinctive features. These features are not however spread uniformly over the whole country but are very frequently regional or even characteristic of a place. Thus every land has regions which through their distinctive climatic, physical, morphological, cultural or other kind of features, constitute the tourist attractions or can be developed to that end. Notwithstanding these territorial individual distinctions, publicity should satisfy the fundamental principles of clarity of objective and uniformity. Clarity of objective in this case signifies that the entire range of national tourist publicity, despite its multifold ramifications, should not show any contradictions, whereas uniformity serves the purpose of creating the impression abroad that all national tourist publicity campaigns are part of a uniform planning. The central idea of publicity planning should be perceptible. It is very rightly mentioned in the *General Theory of Tourism* of Hunziker-Krapf that "the organizational forms of publicity abroad may differ in detail, but there must be a single goal to put national tourism to the fore and the regional and local features on the second plane. These would come into their own once the foreign tourist has made his choice as to the country to be visited."

The tourist publicity can also make use of the brand concept. This, however assumes a certain guarantee of fulfilment. Professor Lisowski has drawn attention to the possibility of creating brands and consequently to the mutual support between brands in the sequence of enterprise-resort-landscape-region country. This mutual support among brands, which can work in both directions, demonstrates still another method which can be followed, namely, that of the most varied publicity combinations through a coupling of the brands. A tourist publicity programme for a country maybe conceived in the following way:

(i) The creation of concepts of satisfaction which, taken together, could form the tourist brand of the country;

(ii) A coordination of all publicity measures of the economic, cultural and tourist institutions of a country in conjunction with a coupling of the brands;

(iii) Constant analysis of satisfactions, market observations and research, as well as publicity effectiveness.

Motivation Publicity **:** The motivating factors of tourism originate in their preponderant majority from the emotional sphere. Consequently, tourism stands out prominently in the world of experience-seeking ideas and conceptions and it can be said that the holidaymaker lives between imagination and reality and the relationship between the two determines his judgement on the land visited. This will be positive in proportion to the extent that reality corresponds to the world of imagination. It may be inferred from this how very important it is for publicity to steer the formation of imagination towards facts as they really exist. This is easiest in the field of comparable satisfactions whereby guiding information on trends may be obtained through a planned investigation of judgements and criticisms—in other words, public opinion research. This publicity based on motivation forces and influencing the imaginative world of the tourists can be referred to as motivation publicity or the irrational approach.

The most intensive publicity is done for recreation, pleasure and cultural travel, and the publicity campaign for this is aimed mainly in producing the result on the imagination that the existing need would find its maximum satisfaction in a particular tourist offer. It has to contend with the horizontal competition of identical or similar appeals and offers. In the application of this method it is essential to have information beforehand about the market facts and conditions like the income-wise classification of the population of different countries, the mental outlook in respect of the presence or absence of the travel lust, and, above all, information about the national habits and preferences, knowledge about the ideas which the average holidaymakers and pleasure travellers associate with the concept of "holiday travel", the destinations which are in the forefront of tourist interest and the reasons thereof.

Within the framework of this method a relatively larger importance is conceded to landscape publicity for relaxation and pleasure travel. In this connection the importance of this subject, in so far as it does not relate to a particularly beautiful landscape or one especially suited for the practice of certain sports, is too much exaggerated. Each region of the globe has a landscape to offer and every one of these landscapes has a particular charm, especially for those whom its special features make it seem strange and therefore worth the experience. To the primary motivations of holiday and pleasure travel, the pressure of the rhythm of our life has added other factors like the escape from the everyday life, freedom from ties and commitments, the urge to adventure, etc. These psychological factors are not taken sufficiently into account and are inadequately utilised in the service of tourist publicity. Publicity for cultural tourism poses lesser problems. It conforms to realities and appeals to a public with an educational background. On the other hand, however, cultural and tourist publicity are so intimately interconnected that there exists the closest coordination.

The second method of tourist publicity is the "reason why" publicity or the rational approach. It extols in the first place the merits or the arguments in favour of visiting the country on behalf of which the publicity has been undertaken and acts in accordance with the principle of suggestion. The form of expression it assumes is the slogan. It is appreciably more strongly competitive which makes it easily liable to fall into the blunder of superlative forms which we come across constantly in tourist publicity.

Publicity Media : The publicity itself is carried out through media whose scope is that there are constantly new possibilities. This is of particular relevance in respect of tourist publicity whose new forms and scientifically based planning in publicity media seem to be constructed as a result of the fact that in general their publicity effect is limited to the visual and auditive senses. Illustration, copy and the spoken word are therefore the primary publicity media for tourism. They are multiplied through the media compounded out of them.

The greatest importance appertains to *illustration,* for it can achieve emotional effects in the reproduction of a landscape and its atmosphere and is also universally understood. Even if one is inclined to accept the psychological argument that every human being only projects his own personality in every consideration, the illustration retains from this standpoint also considerable publicity effectiveness because it is viewed and perceived differently by different persons. Given the differences of individual tastes, the illustration motivation plays a decisive role, for the illustration should be bearer of the emotional contents which it should radiate on the viewer. Consequently the best illustration is just good enough for tourist publicity. It depends on the planning and shaping of the publicity media as to whether the illustration is to be employed in the form of a drawing, a painting, or a photograph. Generally, the photograph is adjudged as possessing a greater objectivity in the statement. On the other hand, an artistic representation can be the expression of cultural activity and hence equally effective as publicity. Illustration can be developed through stylisation into a brand and thus create a concept which is derived from the homogeneousness of circumstances or satisfaction.

With *copy* as a publicity factor, the urgent necessity for originality with the object of giving expression to the publicity idea also arises. The purpose of every publicity media is to arouse and sustain attention. Illustration and copy must therefore create desires. In tourist publicity the tendency towards schematisation is extremely strong and counteracts the necessity for publicity originality. The similarity of the printed publicity material of hotels, travel agencies, tourist resorts, areas and even countries furnishes proof of this. The *spoken word is* of decisive importance in the case of personal publicity. The proper use of the spoken word is difficult but effective. "Words are not only conveyors of thoughts and ideas, but also of emotional contents and consequently they reach not only the intellect but also the psychism of the recipient and are expressed to this end." (Walter Hagemann, *On the Myth of the Mass*). Thus the spoken world helps us to approach the imaginative world of person addressed and this accounts for the importance of the information or sales talk as well as of publicity lectures, radio broadcasts, television speeches and publicity receptions. The spoken word is here supported by the appearance and presence of the speaker, as well as by his psychological capacity to adjust himself to the individual as also a group of listeners.

The three primary publicity media mentioned—illustration, copy and the spoken word—form the basis of the composite publicity media which can suitably be arranged in the following groups:

(i) Printed publicity material,

(ii) Advertising publicity,

(iii) Projected publicity,

(iv) Structural forms of publicity,

(v) Personal publicity.

Printed Material : Printed publicity material in the field of tourist publicity is mainly composed of the publicity leaflet, folder, brochure and poster. The publicity *leaflet* is used among others as inset and enclosure in the case of conveying an information or communicating to the knowledge of the largest possible number of persons. The folder is the most commonly used and the most important medium for tourist publicity. It has numerous forms and multiple variations which leaves unsolved the question of the optimum effective folder. The question culminates in the investigation as to what the recipient expects from a folder, what he looks for in it, what he hopes to find in it and whether the folder corresponds to the imaginative conception of the country or region which it should advertise. The logical conclusion would be to the effect that account should be taken of the mental outlook of the recipient at the time of producing the folder. What actually takes place is that different versions of the folder are printed for different countries. This practice is further confirmed by the production of special folders like the cultural folder and those for motor tourists, mountain climbers, fishing and hunting enthusiasts, etc. These folders deal with the special interests of the recipient and are composed for easy comprehension of the client.

Production of a general folder which has to advertise for a whole country with its variety of attractions, specialities and circumstances, however, is much more complicated. Here, there exists the danger of "too much" as well as "too little", besides the pitfalls of a dry description, superlative forms, over estimation and misappreciation of the points of attraction. A folder is not a travel guide nor a manual of geography. But it must not also be forgotten that the present-day travellers are very often ignorant in the field of tourism and consequently require directions and help as well as information. This renders the setting and composition of the text of an effective general folder a task which has not yet been satisfactorily solved.

The folder must also possess all the necessary qualities required of a good representative—proper appearance, faultless exterior, an unobtrusive and engaging presence, exact information about everything which is offered, truthfulness in assertions and no fanciful exaggerations. The text should never be long-winded. A concrete and concise description containing exact comprehensive information corresponds to the quick rhythm of our time.

The varied nature of the folder results, however, not only from its conception as a general or special folder, but also from the regional and local publicity arrangements. In most countries, there are of course the central publicity organizations, but there are also regional bodies which deal with the tourist interests of a special province or a department. But only in very few cases do such political territorial divisions constitute self-contained tourist areas as well. Consequently, there arises the possibility of joint publicity associations for the promotion and safeguard of the tourist interests of such areas. A classic example of this kind is the joint publicity association of the European Alpine countries which demonstrates how a geographically scenic homogeneity in the form of a publicity unit can complement rationally in the sphere of publicity the various national publicity campaigns. To be adequately effective, however, the publicity medium of the folder needs not only to be well set up, but should also be produced in a sufficient quantity and have a planned distribution.

The brochure is different from the folder in size as well as in content and detail. The importance of the brochure in tourist publicity has not been adequately appreciated and, on account of financial reasons, it has been insufficiently utilized. The brochure offers greater possibilities than the folder to combine with each other publicity and service, suggestion and information.

The poster is another important publicity medium of tourism. The difficulties in respect of the production of the general folder occur especially in the case of the poster. The tourist poster should combine its effectiveness based on psychological factors with the task of expressing the impersonation of a country as a tourist destination working on the limited means at its disposal. The tourist poster further suffers from the fact that there is no well-considered distinction in the production of the poster for application as an interior or outdoor poster. In the majority of cases, there is an interior poster for the premises and show windows of travel agencies and information centres, whose use as an outdoor poster in the streets of large cities is consequently hardly discernible. Nevertheless, it should simultaneously satisfy the imperatives of a good outdoor poster and be designed as an eyecatcher. The problem of publicity is further complicated by the discussion on the pros and cons of graphic and photographic posters.

The publicity journal which is utilized at present by almost every national tourist publicity organization is more representative than all other forms of printed material. As such, it is expensive and therefore limited in its circulation. For the sake of comprehensive coverage, mention may also be made of the printed publicity material which really belongs to the sphere of customer service, like maps, guide books, directories, inserts, etc.

Advertising Publicity : Advertisements can be considered as the best organized publicity medium, even if they require particularly careful preparation and planning. Two principal mistakes are made in the sphere of advertisements. One, consideration is seldom paid to the fact that as a result of the quality of paper and printing errors, the newspaper advertisement can hardly reproduce illustrations in a manner that they have an emotionally suggestive effect. The original pattern must therefore be contrasted with as few half-tones as possible. Two, the one and same original pattern is used in all the selected newspapers, irrespective of the fact that these newspapers often appeal to different social classes. There exist qualitative as well as quantitative readership analyses. The advertisement has a strong effect on the subconscious and must consequently be designed to catch the eye. But it should also express something and try to win over the reader. It needs to be remarked that tourist publicity is also accountable for its share in the wastage of space in the world press through advertisements which are often only empty boasts and leave the informational aspect absolutely out of consideration. The periodical travel supplements of daily newspapers receive the major portion of such advertisements which frequently contain joint publicity for a region or a country. Individual publicity can be very effective in the form of a series of insertions provided a leading idea clearly establishes the link or connection. The selection of the journal should not be determined only by the circulation figures, but also by the influence of the journal within its social class, which again should be examined in relation to its inclination and potentialities for tourism.

Projected Publicity : Projected publicity media comprise film and slide publicity. Of particular importance is the film which is an outstanding publicity medium, not only on account of its representational potentialities, but also because of its suggestive power. The colour film is assuming increasing significance within the framework of tourist publicity. The central idea of the film should be expressible in terms of motion and this accounts for the cardinal rule of all publicity films: short text but plenty of action which should captivate the attention of the spectators and also aim at influencing memory through emotional factors. Publicity effectiveness is a characteristic not only of the purely publicity film, but also of the feature film as well as the instructional or didactic film. In the United States of America and Western Europe the travel film with a commentary known as the "travelogue" has won extensive popularity. Television is a suitable medium to spread the interest in foreign countries and thus serves tourist publicity. In respect of the colour effect, the 8- and 16- mm films make up the greater portion of travel films. Also in their subject treatment, they are often a sequence of shots without any intrinsic connection, simply filmed scenery. Lectures with slides combine the effect of the spoken word and the illustration for direct emotional influence with a generally satisfactory success.

Structural Publicity : Structural publicity comprise all publicity measures which manifest themselves in constructions and structures, as for example, in the establishment and equipment of a tourist publicity office abroad, in participation in fairs and exhibitions, in the preparation of showcases and window displays, etc. There is also the possibility of publicity combinations whereby tourist publicity can be undertaken in conjunction with business publicity. For example, shops selling sports goods, fashion articles, travel accessories, etc., are willing to have such combinations in their show-windows. Similarly at fairs the joint stands of a country procure publicity advantages for tourism because the exhibition as a whole shows tourism in relation to the country and succeeds in creating lasting impressions.

Personal Publicity : Personal publicity in tourism has various forms of application ranging from the informational and sales talk to publicity travel, which serves the need of maintaining contact with the travel industry and to support it in its sales efforts, and includes the publicity lecture. In all these spheres the personal effort holds sway. Also to this category belong interviews, radio broadcasts, television interviews, receptions, etc.

The quantity and choice of the publicity media is determined in accordance with the market and its publicity characteristics like the mental frame of the population, the estimation made of the offers and, finally, the financial resources available. There results consequently a planning based on economic, sociological, psychological and technical factors. Statistics, market analysis and qualitative market research on the one hand and analysis of the product offered as well as publicity research on the other constitute the fundamentals on which an effective publicity planning must be founded.

11

ROLE OF INFORMATION TECHNOLOGY IN TOURISM PROMOTION

In the field of travel and tourism, communication plays a vital role as it is through communication that a potential customers obtains information about a product which, in the final analysis, is a destination which he proposes to visit. Travel and tourism being a service industry the need for not only accurate but rapid information about a destination becomes paramount for the satisfaction of the consumer. In tourism, especially in the area of travel trade and hotel industry across the world, what is being sold and distributed is primarily information about various facilities to be used by the tourist. These facilities and services required by a tourist prior to his departure, during his stay at a destination, and at the time of his departure until he reaches home, make his entire experience worth while.

INTERNET AND TOURISM INDUSTRY

The easy access to information and its worldwide dissemination have been decentralised with Internet taking big strides with each passing day and gaining immense popularity the world over. The invention of internet has opened a new world of information and ushered in a great knowledge era. Its effect has been felt in many sectors like health, commerce, education industry etc. The tourism sector has also felt its effects. Internet, in fact, has brought in a big change in the methods of sales and marketing of different tourism products, reservation systems in airlines, railway, hotels etc.

The Internet today caters to travel activity of all kinds ranging from virtual sightseeing and offering detailed information on travel sights to allowing users to plan their own itinerary, make travel reservations online, offering help with special needs and even maintain online travel diaries. Internet, by way of putting control in the hands of the users and offering discounts unheard of in real life, is fast tempting users to fulfil their travel-related needs online. Virtual sightseeing is the most simplistic form of using the Internet for travel. With users visiting several websites that offer detailed information about travel destinations, and virtually tour these places by pictures and commentaries offered by sites. This is also the fastest and most inexpensive way to go sightseeing today with the only cost being that of Internet access.

COMPUTER TECHNOLOGY IN TOURISM

In the field of tourism, the computer has made entry in a big way. A computer is a managerial tool capable of processing large volumes of data rapidly. It can perform basic arithmetic functions (addition, subtraction, division and multiplication) and logical operations (sorting, ranking and assembling) in a fraction of a second. A computer dispenses results in a large variety of formats. These are capable of repeating programmed instructions almost endlessly without an error, and maintaining a vast database of stored information for possible future use. Today a computer can be put to a variety of uses in the day to day activities.

Although the computers were in use in some way or other in various branches of tourism industry since the early Sixties, today these are considered indispensable. These are extensively used in almost all branches of the travel industry. They are part and parcel of a travel agency and are playing a key role in making the task of providing travel services an easy affair. Computers lately are undertaking, among other jobs, the planning of vacations for an individual and his family through home terminals.

Computer in Airlines

Today almost all the airlines use computers for their entire reservation work. The sudden growth, about forty years ago, in global travel, put a big pressure on the handling of air traffic, especially the passenger traffic for the airlines, both international and domestic. Growth patterns in passenger traffic had begun to indicate that handling reservation manually could not be sustained long without affecting efficiency in the customer service. It was then that a need to computerise passenger reservation systems was felt by the major airlines of the world. IBM took the initiative and developed a computerised reservation system known as Programmed Airlines Reservation System (PARS). This system was developed in the early 1960s. However, PARS was not developed exclusively for or with any one particular airline. The system was designed as an all-purpose software package that would fit the requirements of any domestic airline. It was designed around IBM's new hardware range system 360, which was subsequently to revolutionise the entire computer industry.

The first airline to use PARS was the United States based Continental airlines in the year 1967. This was followed by most major US airlines which used the system making PARS the most popular and successful software product of the time. This was a major achievement for IBM. The system later expanded to meet the needs of several other airlines outside the United States of America resulting in the creation of International Programmed Airlines Reservation System (IPARS). Initially this system was a joint venture between IBM and British Overseas Airways Corporation (BOAC) and aimed at adapting PARS to the needs of airlines that had mainly international operations.

Subsequently, many airlines adopted the system. The international package became almost as much of a standard as PARS. Although many airlines modified the system extensively, IPARS was at the base of most international airlines system. By the late 1960s, the system developed was known as CPARS (C for Compact). This system was followed by a system known as Univac Standard Airline System, USA. With the passing of the years more and more systems developed, incorporating more functions to enable the airlines to have more transactions and instructions. The functions of various systems are basically identical across all airline reservation systems. The differences between them are in areas not apparent to the passengers, such as the flexibility with which they can handle control of space of flights, particularly where multiple classes and multiple sectors are involved.

The popularity of any system to a large extent depends on its coverage and online reservation network. The number of terminals which a system has is also an important consideration. The more the terminals a system has, the larger will be the online reservation network. The number of reservation transactions carried out by a system in a given time is another important aspect. However, it became obvious that the system was too costly, for smaller international airlines developed their own IBM oriented reservation systems in the early 1970s to be considered by an airline before using a system. To sum up, the following main aspects are important to make a system perfect and universally acceptable:

(i) Number of reservation transactions to be handled,

(ii) Data links with other airlines,

(iii) Number of terminals,

(iv) Information processing capacity, and

(v) Data volume capacity.

Computers in Air Cargo

Most of the airlines are now using computers for cargo handling operations as well. The handling of cargo shipments on ground is a costly affair and the cost has been increasing over the years.

Almost 50 per cent of the handling of cargo shipment reflect the cost of manual information processing. Freight rate increases have not kept pace with cost increase, so airlines had either to accept reduced margins or take steps to reduce overheads. Computerisation of cargo has helped reduce costs as this speeds up the handling of information related to consignments and also reduces the time the cargo spends on the ground. The pioneer in cargo computerisation was Alitalia, whose PO 4-cargo system was adopted and modified by many major airlines, such as Swissair, TWA and British Airways. Univac's USAS has a fully developed cargo module. Almost all the major airlines in the world have now adopted one system or another of cargo computerisation.

Advantage to Travel Agents

Today several airlines have developed and adopted sophisticated computer systems for their use. The airlines also make available their system to their appointed sales agents who are equipped with an appropriate terminal and receive the necessary instructions and procedures. Airlines have thus greatly benefited from the use and adaptation of computers. Some of the major advantages of use of computers by airlines include:

(a) high profile applications like passenger reservations;

(b) applications of departure, control and cargo;

(c) accounting, budgeting, forecasting and planning;

(d) engineering management;

(e) cargo management;

(f) revenue accounting;

(g) fare quotations and construction;

(h) ticket printing;

(i) crew scheduling;

(j) crew management; and

(k) yield optimisation

Computer Reservation Systems (CRS)

Computer Reservation Systems (CRS) in recent years has made a major advance in the airline reservation system. Different Computer Reservation systems companies which are global giants in their own rights form a link between the airline and the travel agent by offering online flight bookings and availability details. This system was first introduced in Germany. A system capable of carrying out as many as one thousand reservation transactions every second involving data links with 28 airlines, a host of car hire agencies and hotels and about 20,000 travel agencies in Europe alone was set up in Erding in the southern part of Germany. The System known as "Amadeus" was developed jointly by four airlines-Air France, Iberia, SAS and Lufthansa. The information processing capacity of the mainframe IBM and Unisys computers installed at Erding, the world's largest computer centre involves a data volume of hundreds of thousands of books.

In addition to Amadeus, Galileo and Sabre are two other global giants in Computer Reservation System. CRS can now be used through Internet as well. This has brought the details of online flight booking and availability of seats within the reach of every passenger having an internet connection. The impact of the net can be gauged by the fact that CRS companies have now redesigned themselves as GDSs (Global Distribution Systems). The business is no longer limited to airline bookings alone but covers a broader horizon with value - added travel information.

Role of SITA

Airline industry had, however, laid the foundation for global communication long before the internet was even considered to be of any great value by its pioneers. It has been using networks like SITA 'Societe International de Telecommunications Aeronautiques' set up as early as the year 1949. The role of SITA in airlines automation has been very crucial. Automation is the key to achieving a higher level of productivity in any industry, especially in the airlines industry, and this will continue with more emphasis being put on achieving short-term benefits.

SITA is responsible for providing Data Processing Services. In fact, it is the major supplier of information - handling services for the airline industry. Its aims are to foster efficient telecommunications, data processing and transmission means for all categories of information required in the operation of air transport enterprises, with the specific aim of promoting safe and regular air transport in all countries.

(i) Passenger Reservations

(ii) Departure Control

(iii) Meteorological Data

(iv) Credit Authorisation and Document Verification v) Baggage Tracing (BAGTRAC)

(vi) Share Cargo Service

(vii) Shared Flight Operations data base viii) Flight Planning

(ix) Baggage Handling and Management Service x) Common Customs Interface System

(xi) Fuel Management

(xii) Airline Schedules and Flight Availability database

(xiii) IATA Passenger Tariff Conference Support

SITA is providing a valuable service to the airlines. Almost all the information required in the operation of air transport in the world is being provided to the airlines industry. The range of services. offered by SITA is very extensive and new services are being added as and when these are required. The network today is the world's largest private network serving a large number of countries.

Computer in Hotels

Like in airlines, the computer technology has entered the hotel industry in a big way. A hotel's most crucial internal resource is information and with the use of computers the information is available in a way that saves labour and ultimately increases the profits.

Although computers in the hotel industry started being used as far back as the late 1960s; it was only in the 1970s that the technological advances in computer technology made possible the right combination of compactness and versatility for different sizes of hotels. The lower cost encouraged many individual hotels to install the system. Today computers are installed in large numbers and are widely accepted in the hotel industry. One of the most important factors or its large-scale acceptance in the industry has been its reliability. The computer system has been found to be very reliable in the dissemination of the right kind of information at the push of a button.

Today, the hotel industry is a major market for the computer manufacturers and the software vendors. It has been increasingly realised that the hotel computer systems achieve better internal and external control and, through the use of analysis methods, provide the opportunity to improve the overall profitability of the unit. Like in the airlines, the computers offer substantial advantages for reservation systems in terms of speed and accuracy. The errors are almost negligible.

Application Areas

Hotel systems all over the world have traditionally been divided into the following two main areas:

(1) Front Office Application Areas.

(2) Back Office Application Areas.

Front Office Application Areas incorporate the following:

(i) Reservations

(ii) Registration

(iii) Guest accounting

(iv) Night auditing

(v) Communication operations (telephones, telex, fax).

Back Office Application Areas incorporate the following:

(i) Financial management

(ii) Inventory control systems accounts

(iii) Profit/loss accountss

(iv) General ledger

(v) Credit card verifications

The computer system streamlines the functioning of all the above areas in a hotel set-up. It helps in the smooth functioning of the hotel, better guest relations, increased efficiency of staff and the overall profitability of the hotel. The key to successful operation of a hotel lies in the operation of an efficient information system. With the introduction of computers in the hotel the information system has become more accurate and efficient. The guest has an access to the required information with a push button convenience. Since the computer is used as a communication medium, there is better coordination between various departments. The computer has relieved the staff of many routine jobs enabling them to devote more time and attention to the needs of the guests.

The computers have made guest accounting systems more sophisticated and reliable. It automatically collects and calculates, receipts and payments and consolidates and verifies credit card payments and cash controls. The sales outlets, like restaurants, automatically record the guest's expenditure at the point of sale, while direct electronic links to the telephone system in the guest rooms can monitor guest calls for instant charging to their accounts. The computers have eliminated cumbersome accounting machines often seen at the cashier's desk giving a front office system a modern and sophisticated look, resulting in greater guest satisfaction and adding to the prestige of a hotel.

Back office systems have a large number of areas having great potential for cost control where computers are used to a great advantage for the hotel. With the use of computers, management can monitor the progress of individual restaurants and other sales outlets against targets and budgets which may be set for various items. Daily reports on inventory usage become available by way of organising input from each centre collected at regular intervals throughout the day.

Computer Terminals. The modern day business traveller is increasingly getting used to having a computer in his hotel room. In fact, many such business travellers in countries like USA, Belgium, Holland, France, Switzerland, Germany, Japan, Canada and many other countries are inquiring before booking a room as to whether guest rooms where they are planning to stay have an in-room computer terminal. The computer has thus entered the guest rooms of many hotels in the west and become the latest novelty of a luxury hotel. A number of individual hotels as well as hotel chains have introduced in-room terminals that are hooked by television and telephone into a data system that includes official airline guides, news agencies, stock market agencies, weather bureau, shopping services, travel, club, entertainment guide, electronic games and even job listing features. Access to the computer terminal is gained by the guest by way of punching a credit card number which is charged for their time at the terminals on sliding rates roughly equivalent to those for long distance telephone calls.

HOTELS AND GLOBAL DISTRIBUTION SYSTEMS (GDS)

The hotel industry is today making extensive use of GDS internationally. The GDS basically is a whole gamut of providers who actually started off for the airline industry and then expanded to hotels and car-rental companies. Through GDS, the hotelier can get the customer or a travel agent to make bookings in his hotel. GDS offers more flexibility and instant reservation confirmation.

Computer in Travel Retailing

The profound changes over the years in travel services have made the use of computer technology in retail travel a necessity. The impact of computer technology on travel retailing made itself felt since the beginning of 1980 with the introduction of first-generation agency computer system. It was in the year 1983, that Thomas Holidays, a British company, first used computers. With the success of Thomas Holidays in introducing reservations via Prestel, several more leading tour operators introduced similar systems to sell their 1984 summer programmes. A Prestel set allows travel agents to make reservations with as many principals as agreed to it. The videotex technology which allows tour operators and travel agents to open reservations through Prestel sets is applied to airlines through British Telecom's Skytrack, an automated airline reservation system. This enabled travel agents to make bookings on several hundreds of the world's airlines, using the standard Prestel television set and a keyboard. Prestel was being used for the basics required in the travel industry like finding out airline schedules and fares, making reservations and getting information on a tour operator's holiday packages. The advantage of the system over the travel literature like brochures and books was that the information is automatically updated and only flights or packages that are available are shown.

New Systems-many new systems have been developed lately. There is an intense competition between various systems. Sometimes it becomes difficult for a tour operator or a travel agent to make a choice and decide about the merits and demerits of alternate systems. The new systems which are being used today are Sabre, Apollo, Dacoda, Trav Automation, Worldspan Galileo and Abacus. These systems allow travel agents to find the lowest costs for customers, identify promotions involving frequent flyer miles and free trips and tailormade trips to a customer's specific needs. All these services are available through a push button via the computer terminal.

Computer in Railways

In addition to use of computers by airlines retail agents, travel agents and tour operators, these are also being used directly by the railway systems.

The railway system in Europe and some other countries have now been using computers extensively. In countries like France, Germany, Switzerland and Belgium, to name a few, computers have been in use for over a decade. The most important use of computers in railways, however, is in the area of ticket reservation. The information regarding availability of seats is now available instantly in various networks. Railway systems now use computers for route planning, engineering, accounting, inventory planning and control, purchase and a host of other functions.

The most remarkable use of computer in railways has, however, been made by France. The metro system in Paris is one of the best in the world. France has been making great advances in the technology in its metro system. The latest technological marvel has been achieved beneath the surface of the earth through a concrete cylinder. No one on board is at the controls because there are no controls on board. Instead the sleek good looking aluminium and steel train is being guided by a computer from a distant command centre. Moving at 100 kilometres an hour the train suddenly stops as soon as bright lights appear ahead. Glass doors slide open and the passengers step on an immaculate platform awash in filtered daylight, tastefully decorated with mosaics and sculptures.

The train is the remarkable VAL (Vehicule Automatique Leger), the most ultra-modern futuristic subway system in the world inaugurated in the year 1983 in the Northern French city of Lille. Built by a French high technology giant Matra, the 20-mile network links Lille to the nearby cities. This is considered to be the most advanced automatic subway line in the world. VAL is distinguished from most conventional subway systems by its compact size, speed and computerised operating system. Each car is only 6.75 feet wide and 42.6 feet long as compared to 8 feet by 49.2 feet for a Paris metro car. Each train with two cars carries a normal capacity load of 124 passengers in clean, well-lighted comfort.

The system is operated from a control complex on the outskirts of Lille city. Two rows of television screens form an electronic tableau of the entire system. Four operators can call up images on the video monitors from 250 cameras installed in stations, tunnels and garages. The system's computer is programmed to run the trains at a rate of one train every minute during peak hours and every five minutes at other times. The computer is linked to about 200 microprocessors located in the stations and on board the train. In case of any mishap or accident, VAL operators can stop a train, slow it down or give any of the over 2,000 possible electronic commands.

The trains are equipped with telephones that enable passengers to report any crimes and summon the system's 20-member security force. The driverless system is almost foolproof as is claimed. Indeed, during one of the trial runs, a pigeon alighted on an elevated section of the line, tripping automatic detectors and stopping a train for only ten seconds before its on-board computer ascertained that it was safe to proceed. Railway systems, however, may not be able to indulge in such luxuries for a very long time. However, the importance of computers in railways has been more than emphasised.

12

ROLE OF TOURISM ORGANIZATION

National Tourist Administration (NTAs)

The rapid spread of education led to the desire to find out how people live in other countries. Governments helped in the promotion of tourism by setting up National Tourist Organisations, initially to promote inbound tourism to their country. Some countries actively promoted the concept of overseas travel among their own nationals. Take the case of Japan—this small country of one hundred and twenty million people sends fifteen million tourists to foreign lands every year— more than one out of ten Japanese! The Japanese Government considers it a way of balancing their huge trade surplus with other countries. The Japanese who come to India, for instance, spend money in India. And, the Indian Government which has an unfavourable balance of trade with Japan, can balance the trade gap to some extent.

Over fifty-five million trips to foreign countries are taken by the US citizens every year—and the total US population is a little more than two hundred and eighty million! Domestic tourism, too is an essential part of the lifestyles of Americans, Europeans and the Japanese. Two or three domestic holidays in one year are not uncommon.

Why People Travel

Anybody who travels has a motive of his or her own. On the basis of these motives or purposes, we can divide tourism into distinct categories.

Recreational Travel

The first and foremost is recreational travel. The purpose in this case is recreation—holiday or leisure. People want to get away from the humdrum of everyday life and move to beaches, mountains and the scenic countryside. It has been estimated that seventy-five per cent of international travel in the world and fifty per cent of domestic travel is recreational. According to an Indian Government Survey, done in 1999, seventy-five per cent of foreign visitors come to India for recreation or holiday and the remaining twenty-five per cent come for business, official visits and other purposes.

Adventure and Sports Tourism

The trips undertaken by people for playing golf, tennis, skiing, trekking, mountaineering, etc., fall within this category. Adventure tourism is becoming a popular form of tourism in India. The country offers many opportunities for an adventure holiday and it is becoming more popular.

Cultural Tourism

The third category is cultural tourism. When people are motivated to travel in order to see the cultural heritage of their own country or those of foreign countries, i.e., visit ancient historical monuments, places of religious interest, museums, art galleries, etc., it is termed as cultural tourism. Visits to Varanasi, Haridwar or Rameshwaram are part of cultural tourism.

Health Tourism

The fourth category is that of people who take trips to have medical treatment elsewhere, or to visit places where there are curative possibilities such as hot springs, spas or yoga institutes. This is called health tourism. People travelling to Kerala for ayurvedic treatment or to the USA for major surgeries, fall in this category.

Conference and Convention Tourism

In recent years, two new, but very important categories of tourism have emerged—convention and conference tourism. A large number of people are now travelling within their own country, or abroad to attend conventions or conferences, attending meetings relating to their businesses. The purpose is to gain knowledge through other people's experiences. This is a fast-growing area of travel. In many countries like the USA and Japan, expenditure incurred by company executives on attending business-related conferences overseas, is tax-deductible. If a doctor from the USA or Japan comes to India to attend a medical conference, his expenditure on his Indian trip will be tax-deductible. The Government of India does not extend similar concessions to its professionals as yet.

Incentive Travel

The concept of incentive travel was developed to motivate workers to do a better job. The manufacturing companies or business corporations offer their good workers, sales executives, retailers or wholesalers with rewards of free holidays within the country or overseas which include transportation, hotels, meals and entertainment. People seem to prefer free holidays as a reward, as compared to material gifts like a TV set, refrigerator or a washing machine. In affluent countries, workers often do not need these items as incentives as they have already bought them from their own savings. So, the idea of offering free holidays as an incentive was discovered and has since caught on. Often, the incentive includes free travel, both for husband and wife. Every year, millions of people are travelling as part of incentive travel from their companies in different parts of the world. In countries like the USA, there are travel companies specialising in organising incentive travel only for business corporations. Incentive travel for workers and executives has started in India too—though the scale is as yet modest. Some companies promote foreign tours to neighbouring countries.

Organisation of Tourism

Having determined what makes people travel, we can look at the organisation of tourism in the world. We have discussed in an earlier chapter, the role of travel agents who act as coordinators of different segments of travel.

Travel has become a massive business enterprise. In some countries it has assumed the shape of mass tourism. Imagine, Spain with a population of ten million—had forty-eight million foreign visitors in 2000) had Even in Asia, Singapore has a population of 2.4 million and foreign visitors were seven million in 2000.

Role of Government

Governments, therefore, have to play a key role in the planning, development, regulation and marketing of tourism. Tourism helps every government because it provides employment to the citizens and earns foreign currency for the country. Therefore, practically every government in the world, irrespective of its size, has a NTA.

It may be called a Department of Tourism as in the case of India, a Tourist Promotion Board as in the case of Singapore, a Tourism Authority as in the UK and Thailand or a Tourism Ministry as in the Philippines. The NTAs are involved in planning, development, promotion and administration of tourism. While planning a beach or mountain resort, an NTA tries to make sure that there is no overcrowding, pollution and destruction of historic or archaeological landmarks as a result of the new area development for tourism. To promote tourism, an NTA opens tourist offices overseas to attract foreign tourists to their shores. They also have tourist information offices within their own countries, to provide information to foreign visitors on arrival and also to domestic travellers who wish to travel within their own country.

In India, the Central Department of Tourism has eleven tourist offices in foreign countries and twenty-one within India. In large countries like India, there are several Government tourist organisations. For instance, almost all the twenty-eight State Governments of India and seven Union Territories have their Departments of Tourism and majority of them have Government-owned State Tourism Development Corporations. They operate at State levels. Although most States have their Departments of Tourism and Tourism Development Corporations, the level of tourism development has been uneven. Tourism is a State subject and the Centre cannot enforce its decisions unilaterally on all the States. It was in this context that the National Committee on Tourism (NCT), suggested in 1988 that tourism should be brought on the concurrent list of the Constitution of India, as quoted at the beginning of this chapter. The advantage would be that the Central Government could initiate a legislation in the tourism field for All-India application. Initially State Governments were not interested in tourism development. The Centre had to subsidise the State Governments to open such departments for promotion of tourism. Now most of them are reasonably active and are no longer subsidised by the Centre. The Centre, however, assists them financially to strengthen or streamline their infrastructure where needed.

At the All-India level, there is the public sector—India Tourism Development Corporation (ITDC), with a network of hotels all over India, transport units in various states, a chain of duty-free shops at the international airports and undertaking other tourism-related jobs. Several States have followed the ITDC pattern at their level. Now, a decision has been taken at the Centre that the Government should leave the tourism business to private sector. ITDC is, therefore, in the process of privatisation and the State Governments too are thinking on similar lines. In fact, these Corporations with so much public investments have become a burden on public exchequer, as they are no longer profitable. The Government has to put in money to run them.

World Tourism Organisation

In the organisational chart of tourism, World Tourism Organisation (WTO) is the apex body—representing at world level, the tourism interests of NTAs and working as an affiliate of the United Nations Organisation (UNO). Started as the International Union of Official Travel Organisation (IUOTO) in the first half of the twentieth century, it became an intergovernmental organisation in 1975 and named World Tourism Organisation WTO, for short. Presently, it has a membership.

One hundred and thirty-seven countries and territories. Besides, there are some three hundred and fifty affiliate members like airlines, travel agencies, etc.

WTO provides many services to its members—principal one being the compilation of travel statistics and the publication of books and reports, to help member Governments to plan and develop their tourism. It works closely with several other international organisation with the objectives of helping develop tourism in the world. It offers expert help to developing countries to plan, develop and reorganise their tourism. It strives to improve the quality of tourism education. Presently, its focus is to create environment for sustainable tourism.

India is one of its founding members and is often elected to its Executive Council. Its Chief Executive is called Secretary General. WTO aims to create favourable conditions for free movement of travel in the world. For this purpose, it favours the passport-free travel in the world. To some extent, it has been achieved in all the European countries (EU), where the citizens can travel without visa and passport. Besides, they have introduced a common currency called Euro making travel hassle-free. At present, if a visitor gets visa for one of the eleven European countries, it is valid for all the eleven member countries. WTO is based in Madrid, Spain.

Pacific Asia Travel Association (PATA)

Among other world bodies which sustain and promote international tourism, Pacific Asia Travel Association (PATA) is notable. Although its active members are from the Pacific region, extending from Canada to the Indian sub-continent, (hundred governments, sixty-six airlines and cruise lines. Its presence, etc., worldwide is felt through its more than eighty chapters (seventeen thousand members). It is primarily a marketing organisation, promoting tourism to the Pacific region and assisting member countries in various ways.

Originally established in Hawaii in 1951, it was later headquartered in San Francisco for four decades and is now based in Bangkok, with divisional offices in USA, Australia, Singapore and Europe. It membership exceeds 2000 and consists of governments, airlines, steamship companies, cruise lines, travel agencies, media, etc.

PATA is headed by a Chief Executive and managed by a large Board of Directors, representing many countries. Its annual conventions are a great draw, attracting some one thousand five hundred industry leaders from all over the world. The 2002 Convention was held in New Delhi.

PATA organisation is actively involved in developing ethos for sustainable tourism.

PATA programmes are designed to meet the needs of members, allowing each to remain competitive in the world market place. PATA offers to its members research and marketing services, product development and a variety of educational seminars and workshops.

Besides the above, there are world organisations representing hotels, travel agencies, airlines, transport, etc. We will read about them under different chapters.

In the organisation of tourism, transport is an inseparable element. Tourism transport consists of aeroplanes, motor vehicles, railways, cruise lines, etc. Of course, governments are closely involved in the operation and regulation of the transport system.

Another essential element of tourism is accommodation— hotels, motels, inns, tourist bungalows or lodges, youth hostels, etc., where tourists can stay. (We have a separate chapter on this subject).

Finally, the most important elements are the tourist attractions of a country — scenic beauty, historical monuments, rivers, lakes, parks, mountains, beaches, forests, wildlife, flora and fauna, climate, food and shopping. Tourists come to see and enjoy what a country can offer. Together, all the elements mentioned above, comprise the tourism assets or resources of a country. When these are packaged, the experts call it the 'tourism product' of a country. After all, this is the product a visitor wants to buy. Like manufactured products, the tourism product too has a lot of variety. You can package it in many interesting ways as preferred or demanded by the customers. It may be a holiday on the beaches, a peep into a country's past, a mountain vacation, wildlife viewing or a shopping tour. The visitors have several options and combinations of options at different price ranges.

There is, however, one difference. Tourism is a product which has to be bought unseen. Like manufactured products, you cannot bring them to the customer to see and feel. The customer has to go to it to experience and to feel it! The new technology however, can present to you, on a computor, 'virtual reality' of the tourism product.

India's National Tourist Administration (NTA)

As mentioned earlier, every country sets up its National Tourist Administration (NTA) according to its own requirements. All countries or States of the world, have a NTA, supported and sponsored by the Government of the country. In the western world, most NTAs are sponsored and financed by the Government. In a few countries, private sector also supports it financially and is involved, to some extent, in the management of NTAs. This is not so in India.

The Department of Tourism which manages tourism at the Government level, is wholly dependent on the Government for financial support. No attempt has been made to involve the private sector financially in a supporting role. The private sector is not involved even in an advisory role, though it is sometimes consulted at the discretion of the Goverment.

The argument in favour of private sector participation is that since the private sector is the major beneficiary of tourism promotion undertaken by a Government, it is logical that they share part of the expenditure on tourism promotion and management. The Government of India, in its wisdom, decided not to involve the private sector. Or, when the Government of India mooted the idea of promoting tourism, the private sector was not strong enough to contribute any money. A successful example of the Government and the private sector being actively involved in the NTO affairs is Switzerland, where the private sector contributes almost forty per cent of the expenditure. USA does not have a NTA—it was disbanded in 1995 for economic reasons. Federal Government felt that the private sector should solely promote tourism as they were the primary beneficiaries. And, US tourism has not since looked back.

There were valid reasons for not involving the private sector. When the Department of Tourism was set up in 1958, the travel industry in India was so small and so shy that the Government did not think that the industry could contribute substantially. So, the idea of charging a fee from the industry did not appeal to the decision-makers.

In fact, the private sector in hoteliering and transport was so reluctant that the Government of India had to set up a company in the public sector to build and operate hotels at tourist centres, where the private sector was not willing to invest. Similarly, at major tourist centres like Khajuraho, Varanasi or Jaipur, there was no adequate tourist transport facilities. The public sector company, ITDC with its headquarters in New Delhi, had to step in to operate public sector transport units to provide good transport fleet.

India, therefore, is a unique case history in tourism development.

During the early years of independence, major business houses, except the house of Tatas, did not consider the operation of hotels and restaurants as an honourable business. There were only a few modern hotels in the country and those too run by foreigners. The Government's intervention became necessary to develop the basic infrastructure at major tourist centres to attract foreign tourists. This led to the Government building and operating hotels and transport units, through its public sector organisation like the ITDC all over India. State Tourism

Corporations have followed the same pattern and built budget accommodation and have also operated tourist transport fleets in their respective States.

The tourism scene has changed drastically during the last thirty years and the private sector is now very active in tourism development. Indian hotels in the private sector compare favourably with the best in the world and some of the leading Indian hotel chains are operating hotels in developed countries under their brand name. The Government of India has recognised this fact and decided not to invest any more in the construction of new five-star hotels, leaving the tourism industry totally open to the private sector in India. In fact, there are moves to sell hotels owned by ITDC and Hotel Corporation of India. A few properties were sold in 2002.

India's NTA would, therefore, consist of a Department of Tourism which is a Department of the Ministry of Tourism and also the India Tourism Development Corporation which is a public sector company and implements Government's policy decisions in tourism field. The WTO has a new name for NTOs— the National Tourism Administration—NTAs. They prefer to call it NTA because an Administration has wider ramifications than the Organisation.

The private sector is encouraged by the Department of Tourism to operate tourism facilities under the overall policy guidelines of the Government. In fact, there is an excellent cooperation and understanding between the Department of Tourism and the private sector tour operators, travel agents, transporters and hoteliers in the area of tourism development. Historically, tourism development in India has suffered due to a lack of clear thinking on the part of political decision-makers in the country. Bureaucratic hurdles made it worse.

India became aware of the importance of tourism promotion as early as in 1946. Sir John Sargent, Educational

Adviser to the Government of India, headed a committee to survey the potential of tourism in India and recommended that developing tourist traffic, both internal and external, will be beneficial for India. The recommendation led to the establishment of a Tourist Traffic branch in the Ministry of Transport and Communication, with a network of tourist offices in India and abroad. The branch later transformed itself into a department headed by a director general in 1958. The first overseas tourist office was set up in New York as early as in 1952, followed by similar offices in London, Paris, Frankfurt, Colombo, Melbourne and San Francisco. In retrospect, tourist offices overseas were opened too soon at too many foreign cities without providing them adequate budgetary support and without analysing the availability of adequate infrastructure at home, particularly accommodation suitable for foreigners. Besides, travellers from distant countries like USA, Canada, had a poor image of India as a holiday destination.

Department of Tourism Logo

The establishment of a separate Department of Tourism, helped considerably and the international tourist arrivals which were sixteen thousand in 1951 jumped to over sixteen lakh in 1990, and were twenty-six crore in 2000.

The importance of promotion of tourism for the economic development of India, was realised by the late Prime Minister, Indira Gandhi. She established in 1967, a separate Ministry of Tourism and Civil Aviation under Dr Karan Singh. It was good to tie up tourism with civil aviation, as fast development of tourism is not possible without the total support of the Civil Aviation Ministry, in a country where ninety-eight per cent of foreign visitors come by air. Subsequently, all kinds of experiments have been done with the Tourism Ministry to suit the political needs of the Government in power. At times, the Ministry of Tourism has been separated from Civil Aviation to work in isolation. Later, it was attached to Commerce which made some sense. In 1991, it was tied to Agriculture which made no sense. In 1991, the Tourism and Civil Aviation ministries were again combined under a Cabinet Minister, Madhavrao Scindia. The Deve Gowda Government linked Tourism Ministry with the Ministry of Parliamentary Affairs in 1996. The BJP Government did the same in 1998. Presently, it is attached to Culture which again makes sense. It seems, tourism portfolio is the least attractive for politicians.

The Director General of Tourism in the Department of Tourism, is of the rank of an Additional Secretary and under him are various heads of divisions like planning, publicity, hotels, market research, supplementary accommodation, etc.

Areas of Work

The activities of the Department of Tourism in India, and for that matter, all NTAs anywhere in the world, can be summed up as under the following broad heads:

- Compilation, collection and dissemination of tourist information in India and abroad; attending to enquiries from international tourists, tour operators and travel industry sectors such as airlines, steamship companies and hotels; production of tourist literature—posters, brochures, information directories, tourist guide maps— for wide distribution. Now, most NTAs including India, have set up their websites for travel information so that the people with internet connections can access this information and make their travel decisions. There website have to be updated from time to time;
- Cooperation with international travel and tourist organisations at the Government and non-Government levels;

- Facilitation, such as simplification of frontier formalities in respect of entry of international tourists;
- Development of tourist activities of interest to international tourists;
- Publicity at home and abroad with the object of creating an overall awareness of the importance of tourism;
- Regulation of the activities of various segments of the travel trade, such as hotels, youth hostels, travel agents, wildlife outfitters, guides, tourist car operators and shopkeepers catering to tourist needs; and
- Compilation of statistics and market research on international tourist traffic to India and on its utilisation for effective tourist promotion. Compilation of domestic tourism statistics.

Proposals for Reorganisations

In 1987, the Government of India under the late Prime Minister, Rajiv Gandhi, appointed a high-level National Committee on Tourism under the chairmanship of Mr Mohammed Yunus. The Committee consisted of leading experts on tourism from the Government of India as well as the private sector. A major recommendation of the Committee was the reorganisation of the Department of Tourism, to make it a National Tourism Board like the Railway Board, with considerable autonomy in the implementation of schemes. The other recommendation was to have a cadre of professional tourist officers in the organisation instead of inducting Indian administrative service officers or staff from other ministries.

The recommendations were welcomed by the industry but implementation is not yet on the horizon. The vested interest of the entrenched officers is the major hurdle.

India Tourism Development Corporation (ITDC)

Set up in 1966 as an autonomous public sector corporation, ITDC was entrusted with the task of helping to develop a tourist infrastructure and promoting India as a tourist destination. Over the years, ITDC has been playing a crucial, strategic role in ensuring:

- Proper dispersal of socio-economic benefits of tourism;
- Promoting national integration and international understanding;
- Removal of regional imbalances;
- Generating employment opportunities;
- Augmenting foreign exchange earnings; and
- Acting as a catalyst in the development of tourism by opening up new unexplored tourist areas.

ITDC's present range of operations is diverse. The package of tourist services comprises accommodation, catering, transport, publicity services, duty-free shops, an in-house travel agency— the Ashok Travels—entertainment, conferences, and providing management consultancy services within India and abroad.

Accommodation

The Ashok Group, ITDC's accommodation chain, is the largest in the country and offers accommodation in over three thousand and eight hundred rooms in its thirty-three hotels at twenty-six destinations, ranging from luxury suites to modestly furnished rooms and from beach resorts to moderately priced travellers/ forest lodges. ITDC owns twenty-six hotels—six of its hotels are owned by its subsidiaries.

Accommodation is divided into three categories—Elite (six), Classic (sixteen) and Comfort (eleven). A few of the

ITDC owned hotels have recently been sold to the private sector. It may be mentioned that a few of the ITDC-owned hotels were sold to private sector in 2002.

Management Consultancy

The Corporation's scheme of joint ventures/consultancy collaborations with the State Governments/Tourism Corporations, and private entrepreneurs, has had an enthusiastic response. Several States and private sector organisations have entered into agreements with ITDC, with ITDC operating their hotel properties under a management contract.

Duty-Tree Shops

To facilitate shopping by international passengers, ITDC operates ten duty-free shops and a tax-free shop. The duty-free shops function in the arrival and departure lounges of the international airports of the country—Delhi, Mumbai, Kolkata, Chennai, Thiruananthapuram and Goa. The only tax-free shop is located at Ashok Hotel, New Delhi. Duty-free shops offer a product portfolio of over fifteen thousand. It is currently one of its few profitable areas, others are loss-making including accommodation.

Conferences and Conventions

India's potential for convention tourism has been exploited by ITDC. ITDC's flagship—Ashok Hotel in New Delhi provides good facilities for holding international conferences for a thousand or more people at a time. It is still a popular venue for international conferences in New Delhi.

Ashok Network

The Ashok Network, a centralised reservation service located at New Delhi, with four regional offices covering north, south, east and west India, ensures instant accommodation and transport confirmations for individuals and groups countrywide. An addition to instant bookings/confirmations is Ashok Internet, a hotel-to-hotel reservation system of the Ashok Group.

Ashok Travels and Tours

To provide back-up support to its hotels, the Corporation has its in-house full service travel agency—the Ashok Travels and Tours (ATT). From eleven units, located in various parts of the country, the ATT operates the largest fleet of coaches, tourist cars and air-conditioned limousines.

BIBLIOGRAPHY

- Tourism, Promotion And Power: Creating Images, Creating Identities by N. J. Morgan, Annette Pritchard, ISBN: 0471983411, ISBN-13: 9780471983415, 978-0471983415, Binding: Hardcover, Publishing Date: Jan 1999, Publisher: John Wiley & Sons, Edition: 1970th Edition, Number of Pages: 272, Language: English
- Hospitality: A Social Lens by Conrad Lashley and Alison Morrison.
- Customer Service and the Luxury Guest by Paul Ruffino.
- Fustel De Coulanges. The Ancient City: Religion, Laws, and Institutions of Greece and Rome.
- Bolchazy. Hospitality in Antiquity: Livy's Concept of Its Humanizing Force.
- Jacques Derrida (2000). Of Hospitality. Trans. Rachel Bowlby. Stanford: Stanford University Press.
- Steve Reece (1993). The Stranger's Welcome: Oral Theory and the Aesthetics of the Homeric Hospitality Scene. Ann Arbor: The University of Michigan Press.
- Mireille Rosello (2001). Postcolonial Hospitality. The Immigrant as Guest. Standford, CA: Stanford University Press.

• Clifford J. Routes (1999). Travel and Translation in the Late Twentieth Century. Cambridge, MA: Harvard University Press.

• John B. Switzer (2007). "Hospitality" in Encyclopedia of Love in World Religions. Santa Barbara, CA: ABC-CLIO.

• Immanuel Velikovsky (1982). Mankind in Amnesia. Garden City, New York: Doubleday.

• Barbara Crossette - The Great Hill Stations of Asia. ISBN 0-465-01488-7.

• Kennedy, Dane.The Magic Mountains: Hill Stations and the British Raj (Full text, searchable) Berkeley: University of California Press, c1996. ISBN 0520201884 ISBN 978-0520201880 Product Dimensions: 9.3 x 6.4 x 1.1 inches, Shipping Weight: 1.4 pounds.

• Bradnock, R; Bradnock, R (2004). Footprint India Handbook (13th ed.). Footprint Handbooks. ISBN 1904777007.

• Brown, Percy (1917). Tours in Sikhim and the Darjeeling District (3rd (1934) ed.). Calcutta: W. Newman & Co.. pp. 223. ISBN ASIN: B0008B2MIY.

• Kennedy, Dane (1996). Magic Mountains: Hill Stations and the British Raj. University of California Press. pp. 265. ISBN 0520201884.

• Lee, Ada (1971). The Darjeeling disaster: Triumph through sorrow: the triumph of the six Lee children. Lee Memorial Mission. ISBN ASIN: B0007AUX00.

• Newman's Guide to Darjeeling and Its Surroundings, Historical & Descriptive, with Some Account of the Manners and Customs of the Neighbouring Hill Tribes, and a Chapter on Thibet and the Thibetans. W. Newman and Co.. 1900.

• Ronaldshay, The Earl of (1923). Lands of the Thunderbolt. Sikhim, Chumbi & Bhutan. London: Constable & Co.. ISBN 81-206-1504-2 (Reprint).

- Roy, Barun (2003). Fallen Cicada (2003 ed.). Beacon Publication. pp. 223. ISBN 0732193121X.
- Saraswati, Baidyanath (Ed) (1998). Cultural Dimension of Ecology. DK Print World Pvt. Ltd, India. ISBN 812460102X.
- Singh, S (2005). Lonely Planet India (11th ed.). Lonely Planet Publications. ISBN 1740596943.
- Waddell, L.A. (2004). Among the Himalayas. Kessinger Publishing. ISBN 076618918X.
- TOURISM GEOGRAPHY (Hardcover), Pratap & Prasad , ISBN: 8183290450, ISBN-13: 9788183290456, Publisher: Shree Publishers & Distributors
- TOURISM TRENDS WORLDWIDE (Hardcover) Sharma & Yadav, ISBN: 8183292178, ISBN-13: 9788183292177, Publisher: Shree Publishers & Distributors.
- THE INTERNATIONAL HOSPITALITY BUSINESS (Paperback), ISBN: 8179927458, ISBN-13: 9788179927458, Publisher: Jaico Publishing House.
- UNDERSTANDING THE HOSPITALITY CONSUMER (HOSPITALITY, LEISURE AND TOURISM) (Paperback), WILLIAMS, ISBN: 0750652497, ISBN-13: 9780750652490 , Publisher: Elsevier.
- TOURISM AND HOSPITALITY MANAGEMENT (Hardcover), Kandari & Chandra, ISBN: 8188658464, ISBN-13: 9788188658466, Publisher: Shree Publishers & Distributors.
- TRAVEL AND TOURISM MANAGEMENT (Hardcover) by Kandari & Chandra, Published by Shree Publishers & Distributors,, ISBN: ISBN-13: 9788188658732.
- TRAVEL TOURISM AND HOSPITALITY (Hardcover), Kandari & Chandra, ISBN: 8188658758, ISBN-13: 9788188658756, Publisher: Shree Publishers & Distributors.
- TOURISM AND SUSTAINABLE DEVELOPMENT (Hardcover), Kandari & Chandra, ISBN: 8188658995,

ISBN-13: 9788188658992, Publisher: Shree Publishers & Distributors.

• TOURISM : SUSTAINABILITY AND GROWTH (Hardcover) by Kandari & Chandra, ISBN: 818865843X, ISBN-13: 9788188658435, Publisher: Shree Publishers & Distributors.

• FINANCIAL MANAGEMENT OF TOUR AND TRAVEL (Hardcover), Dinesh Kaushik, ISBN: 8189000802, ISBN-13: 9788189000806, Publisher: Axis Publications.

• ECO-TOURISM (Hardcover), Kandari & Chandra, ISBN: 8188658979, ISBN-13: 9788188658978, Publisher: Shree Publishers & Distributors.

• TOURISM IN THE PACIFIC (Paperback), ISBN: 0415125006, ISBN-13: 9780415125000, Publisher: Taylor & Francis Ltd.

• TOURISM MARKETING, Dr B. K Kapoor, ISBN: 9788089232, ISBN-13: 9789788089230, Publisher: Axis Publications.

• TOURISM MANAGEMENT (Hardcover), J.S. Bajwa , ISBN: 8131300471, ISBN-13:9788131300473, Publisher: APH Publishing Corporation.

• PROFILES OF INDIAN TOURISM (Hardcover) by Shalini Singh, ISBN:8170247489, ISBN-13: 9788170247487, Publisher: APH Publishing Corporation.

• FOOD AND BEVERAGE SERVICE (Hardcover) by Anil Sagar, ISBN: 8176482420, ISBN-13: 9788176482424, Publisher: APH Publishing Corporation.

• CRISIS MANAGEMENT IN THE TOURISM INDUSTRY (Hardcover) by Dirk Glaesser, ISBN: 0750659769, Publisher: Butterworth-Heinemann.

INDEX